ARDEN PERFORMANCE EDITIONS

W9-BON-348

A MIDSUMMER
NIGHT'S DREAM

ARDEN PERFORMANCE EDITIONS

Series Editors: Michael Dobson, Abigail Rokison-Woodall and Simon Russell Beale

Published titles
A Midsummer Night's Dream edited by
Abigail Rokison-Woodall
Hamlet edited by Abigail Rokison-Woodall
Romeo and Juliet edited by Paul Menzer

Further titles in preparation
Macbeth edited by Katherine Brokaw
Much Ado About Nothing edited by Anna Kamarilli
Othello edited by Paul Prescott
Twelfth Night edited by Gretchen Minton

ARDEN PERFORMANCE EDITIONS

A MIDSUMMER NIGHT'S DREAM

Edited by
ABIGAIL ROKISON-WOODALL

THE ARDEN SHAKESPEARE
LONDON • NEW YORK • OXFORD • NEW DELHI • SYDNEY

THE ARDEN SHAKESPEARE
Bloomsbury Publishing Plc
50 Bedford Square, London, WC1B 3DP, UK
1385 Broadway, New York, NY 10018, USA

BLOOMSBURY, THE ARDEN SHAKESPEARE and the Arden Shakespeare logo
are trademarks of Bloomsbury Publishing Plc

First published 2017
Reprinted 2019 (twice), 2020 (twice)

A catalogue record for this book is available from the British Library.

A catalog record for this book is available from the Library of Congress.

ISBN: PB: 978-1-4742-4519-7
          ePDF: 978-1-4742-4521-0
          eBook: 978-1-4742-4520-3

Series: Arden Performance Editions

Typeset by RefineCatch Limited, Bungay, Suffolk
Printed and bound in Great Britain

To find out more about our authors and books visit www.bloomsbury.com
and sign up for our newletters.

CONTENTS

Preface   vii

Series Introduction   ix

A Note on Metre   xxiii

Introduction   xxix

Suggested Further Reading   xlvii

Dramatis Personae   xlix

A MIDSUMMER NIGHT'S DREAM   1

PREFACE

The impulse for the Arden Performance Editions came from a shared interest in creating an edition of Shakespeare that would best serve actors in a rehearsal room and also students in the classroom seeking to bring the text from page to stage. We wanted to provide a reliable text of each play, drawn from the scrupulously-prepared Arden Third Series editions and thus informed by the latest textual and historical scholarship, but newly thought-through, reannotated and redesigned with the practical needs of theatre-makers in mind.

This was partly about convenience – in terms of weight, print size, placement of notes, and concision of glossing. It was also about empowering actors and readers by making easily visible the sorts of editorial choices about lineation, punctuation and textual variants that can be less easy to discern in more lavishly-edited scholarly editions. We wanted to provide a clear sense of the available choices in terms of viable textual variants (where differing versions of a play survive from Shakespeare's own time), without getting embroiled in generations-old academic debates about whose emendations to which Elizabethan printer make the most sense. We also wanted it to be easy for our actor-readers to identify cases of ambiguous lineation, where different later editors have chosen to divide Shakespeare's verse-lines at different places: these editorial choices can prove misleading to an actor looking for certain 'clues' to delivery in the structure of the verse.

The punctuation of these editions was a matter of debate. We began by thinking that we might remove some of the bulky punctuation included in most modern editions, stripping it back to something more akin to that of some of the editions published in Shakespeare's lifetime – sparse punctuation that is often perceived as more 'actor-friendly'. However, it soon became clear that this was going to be difficult to implement across the board. Whilst we could have punctuated *Hamlet* based on the relatively sparse punctuation of the second quarto (1604), the same could not have been said of *The Tempest*, where the only extant early printed text is the heavily punctuated First Folio (1623). Here any choice of a minimal 'Elizabethan-style' revision to the punctuation would have been merely arbitrary, and would in many places have made Shakespeare's meaning less easy to discern rather than more so. In practice we have settled for the punctuation of the Arden Third Series editions, which is principally designed to convey sense to a reader. Actors who find this too cumbersome are encouraged to take the commas and semicolons supplied throughout these editions lightly. In the preparation of copy for Elizabethan printers and in the setting of that copy in the presses, it was usually scribes and compositors rather than playwrights who made decisions about where such punctuation marks appeared. In the theatre, such choices are still up to actors. We hope that these editions will make them clearer.

We hope these editions illuminate and explain Shakespeare's texts without imposing any specific ideas about how to inhabit, perform, read or enjoy them. Our aim throughout has been to set our actor-readers' imaginations free.

Thanks to:
Margaret Bartley who had faith in the idea and has worked tirelessly to see it realized.

The Bloomsbury Arden team for their support and expertise.

The Arden Third Series volume editors whose expertise has provided us with authoritative, modernized editions.

Ralph Alan Cohen, The American Shakespeare Center, our Series Advisor.

Michael Dobson, Abigail Rokison-Woodall,
Simon Russell Beale

SERIES INTRODUCTION

Actors working with modern editions often run up against editorial decisions which may affect their interpretations. Editorial principles for lineation and punctuation are not always made explicit, and are frequently consigned to the discursive notes at the beginning or end of the text. The principles for the selection of particular textual variants vary between editions, and the possible choices available to the actor are not always immediately apparent.

This edition seeks to open the text to actors, making clear those instances where there is a genuine choice in terms of textual variants, and leaving the lineation of the text as open as possible.

PUNCTUATION

- The punctuation of this edition is that of the Arden 3 text, since this is designed to convey the sense most clearly.

- No extant text of Shakespeare represents the author's own punctuation.

- Even the punctuation of early quarto editions thought to have been printed from an authorial manuscript is likely, for the most part, to have originated with the scribes and compositors who were responsible for the transcription and printing of these copies.

- In some cases the punctuation in the Folio is as heavy, or heavier, than that of many modern edited texts.

- With this in mind it seems arbitrary to pick a particular early modern text from which to take the punctuation – this creates as many problems as it solves.

- Actors are not obliged to follow the punctuation of the text in delivery. They may find that it is sometimes better to phrase according to the metre.

- In cases where the punctuation of an early quarto or Folio seems particularly useful or interesting in providing an indication of a character's mood or thought patterns, we provide a facing page note.

LINEATION

- The lineation of the edition is, again, based on that of Arden 3.

- However, in cases where the lineation is ambiguous, a facing-page note to this effect is added.

- Where the metrical connection between lines seems unambiguous – so-called shared lines – this edition follow George Steevens and editors since 1793 in indenting the second part of the line in order to make the connection visually explicit.

- In cases where three part-lines succeed one another, each pair appearing to have an equal metrical claim to linkage, this edition does not follow the common editorial practice of representing such lines as one shared and one short line. Instead we make the ambiguous metrical connection apparent by indenting both the second and third portions of the line, thus:

MARCELLUS
 Holla Barnardo!
BARNARDO Say, what, is Horatio there?
HORATIO   A piece of him

          (*Ham.* 1.1.17)

- In cases where one of the lines might be regarded as an overlapping or interjecting line outside the metrical structure of the scene, we add a note on the facing page, as in this example from *Hamlet*:

HAMLET
> . . . A cut-purse of the Empire and the rule,
> That from a shelf the precious Diadem stole
> And put it in his pocket.

GERTRUDE   No more.

HAMLET   A King of shreds and patches,

>   (*Ham.* 3.4.97–100)

Hamlet's lines could be considered to be continuous with Gertrude's line overlapping. This form of overlap would have been easily indicated to the Renaissance actor working from a cue part by giving the actor playing Hamlet a continuous speech, and the actor playing Gertrude the cue-line 'in his pocket'.

- Where more than three short lines succeed one another and the metrical connection is ambiguous, all lines are aligned to the left-hand margin and a note is added.

- This form of lineation is partly motivated by historical evidence suggesting that early modern actors, because of the nature of the scripts they worked with, would not have been able to see the metrical connections between their lines and those of other speakers, and are therefore unlikely to have distinguished between full-line and short-line cues in their delivery.

METRE

- Whilst the dominant metre of Shakespeare's verse is iambic pentameter (five feet per line), Shakespeare increasingly varies this metre, introducing other feet. A note on the metre with more details of metrical variants is provided in the section 'A Note on Metre'.

Long and short lines

- Although most lines have ten (or eleven) syllables, some lines have more or less than this.

- In some instances it is possible to make a line scan as a line of pentameter by eliding a word, for example 'even' being pronounced as one syllable (sometimes represented in editions as e'en).

- In other cases the metre suggests the expansion of a word, for example, the pronunciation of intermission as five syllables (**in**-ter-**miss**-i-**on**).

- Facing-page notes are given to alert the actor to such metrical indications.

- The notes indicate the equivalent number of syllables suggested by the metre; for example:

even (equiv. 1 syl.)

in-ter-**miss**-i-**on** (equiv. 5 syl.)

- Bold type in these notes indicates stressed syllables.

- In some cases what appears to be a long line can be scanned by substituting an anapest for an iambic foot. In such cases a facing-page note is provided. The section 'A Note on Metre' explains the use of the anapest.

- Finally, some lines cannot be easily scanned as pentameters. In such cases we provide a facing-page note indicating that a line is either short or long. There is no expectation that the actor will change his or her delivery.

- In a few cases a line of nine syllables is clearly missing the first stressed syllable. This is called a 'headless foot' and its presence is noted in a facing-page note.

- In some cases the verse form suggests that a word might be pronounced differently from its usual sound in both present-day and early modern everyday speech.

- In the case of words ending in 'ed', the metre sometimes suggests that the ending should be pronounced as an extra syllable. In such cases the 'ed' ending is given a grave accent – èd – viz. examinèd.

- In cases where the metre does not suggest the pronunciation of the word-ending as a separate syllable, the word is ended with 'd – viz. examin'd.

- The aim throughout is to inform and assist rather than to dictate, and the pronunciation of words is, of course, a matter of individual choice.

PRONUNCIATION

- In cases of unusual words or names, this edition provides a guide to pronunciation in a facing-page note (preceded by 'Pron.').

- Pronunciation of character names is given in the *Dramatis Personae* (and not thereafter in the text).

- In cases where a word is used several times, varying in scansion according to the metre, a note is given in the Introduction (and not for each use in the text).

TEXTUAL VARIANTS

- Some of Shakespeare's plays were printed in two or more different early editions.

- Thirty-six of Shakespeare's plays were published in the First Folio of 1623. Prior to the publication of the Folio, eighteen of these plays had appeared individually in quarto form.

- *Pericles* and *The Two Noble Kinsmen* – not included in the First Folio – were also printed in quarto form.

- Some of the quarto texts differ little from their Folio counterparts. In other cases the differences are substantial.

- In most cases there are some variations in terms of individual words.

- Some of these are merely representative of an error of transcription or printing.

- However, in other cases differences between the early texts present the actor with a genuine choice. In such instances we make clear the textual variants in a facing-page note.

Q – indicates a quarto variant

F – indicates a Folio variant

Q1 – First quarto, Q2 – Second quarto, etc.

F1 – First Folio, F2 – Second Folio, etc.

Qq – all authoritative quartos

- In a few cases the quarto and Folio texts contain obvious errors – the result of misreadings, damaged copy or error. In many cases these were emended by eighteenth-century editors. Where this is the case, a facing-page note makes the editorial emendation apparent:

Rowe – Nicholas Rowe, 1709

Pope – Alexander Pope, 1725

Theobald – Lewis Theobald, 1733

Hanmer – Thomas Hanmer, 1744

Warburton – William Warburton, 1747

Johnson – Samuel Johnson, 1765

Capell – Edward Capell, 1768

Steevens – George Steevens, 1773

Malone – Edmond Malone, 1790

- Each individual edition provides a clear summary of the variant texts and notes any major textual differences.

SCENE LOCATIONS

- About two-thirds of scenes in Shakespeare plays written for the Globe are unlocated. No indication is given of their precise locale even in the dialogue, and in no early text does an announcement on the page at the beginning of a scene specify where it is taking place.

- When location is important to a scene, Shakespeare usually has characters (or a chorus) vocalize it – for example, 'Well, this is the forest of Arden' (*As You Like It*, 1.4.12), 'The orchard walls are high and hard to climb' (*Romeo and Juliet*, 2.2.63), 'Unto Southampton do we shift our scene' (*Henry V*, 2.0.42).

- As a result, we have resisted the temptation to provide arbitrary locations for scenes.

- The setting of a scene is clearly a matter for each individual production to define (or to leave as ambiguous).

- In texts where scenes have clearly defined locations, these are discussed in the introduction to that edition.

STAGE DIRECTIONS (SD)

- This edition follows the stage directions given in the Arden 3 text.

- The early printed texts of Shakespeare's plays contain relatively few stage directions.

- Where stage directions do not appear in the early texts but have been added by subsequent editors, they are presented in brackets – i.e. [*Exit PHILOSTRATE*].

- There are a few cases in the Folio or quarto texts where a character is instructed to enter in a stage direction, but does not speak. In such cases we provide a facing-page note. The decision as to whether a character who does not speak is to be included in the scene is a matter for each production to determine.

- There are a number of instances in the Folio text of what have been termed 'anticipated entrances' – where a character is instructed to enter on stage before they are required to speak. These entrances may simply indicate the time taken for an actor to get from the back to the front of the Globe stage. However, in some cases they suggest an interesting possibility that a character is seen by the onstage characters before they speak or overhears the onstage action. In such cases we provide a facing-page note indicating the position of the entrance in the Folio (or occasionally Quarto) text.

YOU AND THOU

- In early modern England the pronouns 'you' and 'thou' each served a distinctive function, much like the French equivalents 'vous' and 'tu'.

- Having earlier been the standard form of address, 'thou' became a 'special' pronoun, used affectionately to indicate closeness between speakers, used derogatively in order to patronize or vituperate, and used when addressing allegorical figures, gods or the dead.

- As well as being the plural, 'you' was the more respectful form of address.

- Individual editions contain a brief note on the most significant uses of personal pronouns in the play.

RHETORIC

- Rhetoric – the art of verbal persuasion, studied and codified since classical times – exerted a powerful influence on Elizabethan writing, and rhetorical devices abound in the work of Shakespeare and his contemporaries.

- Some of the most common rhetorical devices are alliteration, assonance, various patterns of repetition, and especially antithesis, which Shakespeare uses frequently to balance lines and to counterbalance clauses, setting light against dark, love against hate, and so on.

RHYME

- Shakespeare uses rhyme in various ways in his plays, the most common being for songs and for rhyming couplets – sometimes isolated, sometimes formed into speeches.

- In Shakespeare's early plays, one of the most common uses of the rhyming couplet is to end a scene.

- In his later plays these final couplets are less common. Sometimes a scene finishes on a couplet followed by a short line which gives a different momentum to an exeunt.

- Couplets are also used to end speeches, adding a flourish to their conclusion.

- A further use of rhyme comes in the form of aphorisms, where characters seem to be coining or citing pithy generalizations.

- One difficulty for the modern actor is that changes in pronunciation from the early modern period to the present day mean that lines that once rhymed do so no longer.

- In such cases we provide a facing-page note. An actor is free to ignore the rhyme and pronounce the words as they are commonly spoken or to employ a deliberately antiquated delivery in order to point up the rhyme.

VERSE AND PROSE

- Most of Shakespeare's plays are written in a mixture of verse and prose.

- *Henry VI Parts 1* and *3* (c. 1591), *Richard II* (c. 1595) and *King John* (c. 1596) are written entirely in verse.

- *The Merry Wives of Windsor* has the highest proportion of prose – 90%.

- The characters who most often speak prose are:
  - servants, clowns, sailors and workingmen;
  - upper-class characters coming into contact with working-class characters;
  - foreign characters;
  - drunken characters;
  - characters experiencing madness and psychological imbalance;
  - characters in disguise.

- Prose is commonly used for lesser subject matter than verse and for comic dialogue.

- The majority of letters and proclamations are in prose.

- A move from verse to prose within a scene often marks a significant change in tone. There is an increasing tendency in the process of Shakespeare's career to modulate from one medium to another within a scene.

Where a scene moves from verse to prose or vice-versa this is indicated in a facing-page note.

- During Shakespeare's career his use of prose becomes more varied, and prose is more often spoken by characters from the upper classes.

- It is sometimes difficult to distinguish between verse and prose. This may be deliberate. In such cases we provide a facing-page note.

- Each individual edition provides a summary of the key uses of verse and prose in the play.

SOURCES

- Many of Shakespeare's plays are based on pre-existing sources – ancient texts such as Plutarch's *Parallel Lives*, classical poems, historical chronicles, earlier plays and stories.

- Shakespeare regularly made alterations to his source material, either in order to make it more theatrical, to make it more shocking (as in the case of the tragic ending which only Shakespeare gives to the well-known legend of King Lear), or to make it more politically and socially relevant.

- It can be misleading for an actor to explore the source material for a text as a means of discovering more about a character, particularly in the case of historical figures: an attempt to play Shakespeare's Richard III as though the play were a documentary about the historical Richard III, for example, is likely to produce contradictory and undramatic results

- Nevertheless, it can be interesting to note the changes made, and to know some of what Shakespeare was deliberately leaving out or transforming.
- As a point of interest, each edition provides a list of key sources for the play.
- Where there is a clear and significant source for a particular reference, we provide a facing-page note in the text, marked 'Source'.

Proverbial sayings

- Shakespeare's characters often use proverbs.
- Some characters make conscious use of common sayings – sometimes to the point of cliché.
- Others deliberately manipulate well-known aphorisms.
- Since it seems useful for actors to be aware of when a character is consciously using proverbial language, key proverbial sayings are marked 'Prov.'.

Biblical allusions

- Characters in Shakespeare's plays frequently quote from or refer to the Bible.
- Such references would have been more familiar to early modern actors and audiences.
- Again, it seems useful for actors to be aware of when their character is invoking the Bible.
- Biblical allusions are marked 'Bib.'.

LIST OF ABBREVIATIONS

Bib. – biblical
equiv. – equivalent to

Intro. – Introduction
Myth – Key figures of Classical mythology
Pron. – pronunciation
Prov. – proverbial
Punct. – punctuation
SD – stage direction
SP – speech prefix
syl. – syllable/ syllables

Michael Dobson, Abigail Rokison-Woodall,
Simon Russell Beale, *Series Editors*

A NOTE ON METRE

Shakespeare's basic metre is iambic pentameter. Iambic pentameter is made up of five feet (a foot being a unit of verse made up of stressed and unstressed syllables) comprising an unstressed syllable followed by a stressed syllable, annotated thus: u /. A regular line of iambic pentameter is scanned as follows:

u /   u / u /   u /   u /

HERMIA

I would my father look'd but with my eyes.

(A Midsummer Night's Dream, 1.1.56)

Although iambic pentameter forms the basis of Shakespeare's metre, his metrical line admits a number of variations, particularly as his career progresses.

The essential difficulty with the introduction of iambic pentameter to the English language was that English language has inherent stresses. We pronounce 'inherent' as 'in **her** ent' not '**in** her **ent**', for example. When iambic pentameter was first introduced into the English language, many poets could see little alternative but to use it in a regular fashion. George Gascoigne, in his 'Certayne Notes of Instruction concerning the making of verse of rhyme in English' (1575), one of the first English publications on metre, instructs the poet that 'euen in this playne foote of two syllables [he or she should] wreste no woorde from his natural and vsuall sounde' (George Gascoigne, 'Certayne Notes of Instruction concerning the making of verse or rhyme in English', in *The posies of George Gascoigne Esquire* (London, 1575, 50)).

He gives the following example:

> I understand your meanying by your eye
> Your meaning I understand by your eye

commenting that,

> in these two verses there seemeth no difference at all, since the
> one hath the very selfe same woordes that the other hath, and
> yet the latter verse is neyther true nor pleasant, and the first
> verse may passe the musters.
>
> (Gascoigne, 50–1)

And yet Shakespeare and his contemporaries could not always
compose sentences in alternate stresses (this would have
become tedious), and thus they began to introduce variants,
three of the most common being:

1. The trochee – a foot composed of a stressed syllable followed
   by an unstressed syllable (/ u). An example might be the
   first foot of this line:

   /   u   u / u   / u / u /

   Friendship is constant in all other things

   (*Much Ado*, 2.1.160)

2. The Spondee – a foot composed of two stressed syllables
   (/ /). An example might be the first foot of this line:

   /   /   u /u / u   / u /

   Hence! home, you idle creatures, get you home:

   (*Julius Caesar*, 1.1.1)

3. The Anapest – a foot composed of two unstressed syllables
   followed by a stressed syllable (u u /). An example might be
   the first foot of this line:

   u u / u   / u / u / u   /

   Be it so she will not here, before your Grace,

   (*A Midsummer Night's Dream*, 1.1.39)

Many lines in Shakespearean drama that might otherwise be considered irregular can be scanned by substituting one of these metrical feet for an iamb. In some cases the scansion is subjective. Whilst one person may wish to speak the following line:

HORATIO
What, has this thing appear'd again tonight? (Ham. 1.1.19)

scanning 'What, has' as an iamb (with the stress on 'has'), another might wish to scan it as a trochee (with the stress on 'What') and another as a spondee (with the stress on 'What' and 'has').

In the case of trochees and spondees, the substitution of one of these feet for an iamb does not affect the overall syllable count of a line, and thus we do not regularly give an indication of where we feel such feet might be present.

There are a few instances in Shakespeare's work of full lines of trochaic rather than iambic metre. Most frequently these are present in Shakespeare's 'magic' metre – when he is writing dialogue for the fairies in *A Midsummer Night's Dream* or for the witches in *Macbeth*. However, they sometimes occur elsewhere in the plays, and their presence is noted, for example, in *Romeo and Juliet*:

Romeo, humours, madman, passion, lover,

(2.1.7)

However, the anapest incorporates an extra syllable into a line, making it appear irregularly long if one does not acknowledge the possibility of this foot. In cases where a line can be made to scan as five feet by the inclusion of an anapest, we note this in a facing-page note.

A more extreme example, similar to an anapest, is the quartus paeon, a foot which comprises three unstressed syllables followed by a stressed syllable (u u u /). In most cases the presence or otherwise of a quartus paeon is ambiguous, and a line might equally be scanned as a deliberate hexameter (six feet), as in the following example.

This line can be scanned with the third foot (quish-er as by) as a quartus paeon:

u / u   / u u   u / u /   u /
Had he been vanquisher, as by the same co-mart

(*Hamlet*, 1.1.90)

or as a deliberate hexameter:

u   / u   / u / u / u /   u /
Had he been vanquisher, as by the same co-mart

(*Hamlet*, 1.1.90)

Some critics suggest that hexameters are rare and that it is preferable to attempt regularization where possible (E.A. Abbott, *A Shakeseparean Grammar*, 397). Others freely admit the presence of hexameters (George T. Wright, *Shakespeare's Metrical Art*, Chapter 9).

There are sometimes a number of possible ways of scanning a particular line. In the following example, either the second (-lling shall not lack) or third (Let us go in) foot might be scanned as a quartus paeon, or the line can be regarded as a hexameter (with a feminine ending).

God willing shall not lack. Let us go in together

(*Hamlet*, 1.5.192)

In other cases, scanning a line as a hexameter seems the only logical choice:

He heareth not, he stirreth not, he moveth not;

(*Romeo and Juliet*, 2.1.15)

SHORT LINES

Headless lines

A common variation on the regular iambic pentameter line is that of the 'headless' line. A fairly common metrical device in Shakespeare's work, the headless line is a line that is missing the first unstressed syllable:

(u) / u / u / / u u /
Melted as the snow, seems to me now

> (*A Midsummer Night's Dream*, 4.1.166)

(u) / u /
HORATIO   Where, my lord?

u / u / u / u
HAMLET   In my mind's eye, Horatio.

> (*Hamlet*, 1.2.185)

Missing beats at the caesura

A further variation on the short verse line is the line in which a beat appears to be missing at the caesura. The caesura is the strong mid-line break in a line of verse, often marked by the end of a phrase or sentence.

If the missing beat is an unstressed beat, this is termed a 'broken-backed line', for example:

u / u / (u) / u / u /
To hide the slain?   O, from this time forth

> (*Hamlet*, 4.4.66)

Other lines may be missing a stressed syllable at the mid-line caesura:

```
u   /  u   /   u (/) u  /   u /
```
As he would draw it. Long stay'd he so;

(Hamlet, 2.1.87)

FEMININE ENDINGS/ TRIPLE ENDINGS

The regular iambic pentameter line consists of five feet, each made up of an unstressed syllable followed by a stressed syllable. One of the most common variations on this line is the presence of what is commonly termed a feminine (or unstressed) ending. A feminine ending consists of an extra unstressed syllable at the end of the ten-syllable line, for example:

```
u   / u / u /    / u u  /    u
```
To be, or not to be – that is the question;

(Hamlet, 3.1.54)

Occasionally a line ends with two additional unstressed syllables – termed a triple ending:

```
u   / u    / u /    u /   u /   u u
```
And tediousness the limbs and outward flourishes.

(Hamlet, 2.2.91)

In this case, 'flourishes' may be seen as equivalent to two syllables.

INTRODUCTION

THE VARIANT TEXTS

A Midsummer Night's Dream was written in 1595/6.

There are four key early printed texts:

- First Quarto (Q1) – published in 1600, from Shakespeare's own manuscript ('foul papers').
- Second Quarto (Q2) – published in 1619 (wrongly dated 1600), printed from the first quarto.
- First Folio (F1) – published in 1623, printed from a copy of the second quarto which had been annotated with reference to a promptbook, i.e. a copy of the play which had been used in the theatre to regulate a performance.
- Second Folio (F2) – published in 1632 – printed from the First Folio, with some corrections.

The word 'quarto' refers to the format of the text – a quarto is made up of large sheets of paper that have been folded twice, each printed page being a quarter of a full sheet. A quarto is usually around 8.5 inches in height. Only half of Shakespeare's plays were printed in quarto form during his lifetime. That *A Midsummer Night's Dream* was printed in 1600, 1619 and 1632 is an indicator of its enduring popularity.

The word 'Folio' refers to a book of around 15 inches in height, made up of full sheets of paper which have been folded in half. The First Folio is thus about twice the size of the early printed quartos. The folio format was, in general, only used for prestigious books – works by leading theologians, philosophers and historians.

The First Quarto (closest to the authorial text) provides the textual basis for all three texts.

Differences between the First and Second Quarto, whether these be new errors or the correction of existing ones, are likely to derive from printers rather than from either Shakespeare or his theatrical colleagues.

Differences between F and Q2 may result from the consultation of a promptbook, and thus may represent deliberate changes made to the text by Shakespeare or his colleagues over the course of its early performances.

This chart provides an indication of the origins of the texts:

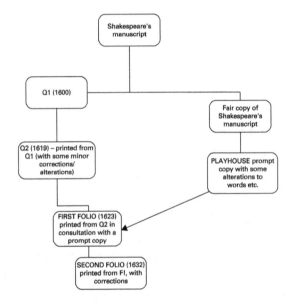

THIS TEXT

The text used in this edition is based on the Arden 2 text, edited by Harold F. Brooks, which is predominantly based on Q1. The punctuation of the text is modernized.

MAJOR TEXTUAL DIFFERENCES

The differences between the variant texts are relatively few, and in most cases simply take the form of a plural rather than a singular, the substitution of a synonym, or – most commonly with this text – a change in word order. Where Q2 and F agree against Q1, then it is likely that the alteration in word order is a printing house error in Q2 replicated by the Folio. Where F differs from Q1 and Q2, the difference may be the result of error or may reflect a deliberate alteration recorded in the playhouse prompt copy.

In a few places an apparent error in the original text has been replicated across all three texts. In such cases later editors have emended the text for the sake of sense, for example, 'And then the moon, like to a silver bow / New-bent in heaven …' (1.1.9–10), where 'New-bent' is a correction (first offered by the editor Nicholas Rowe in 1709) for the Qq/F 'Now bent'.

In the relatively few cases where such emendations are commonly accepted by modern editors, they are adopted here, with a facing-page note.

Some major editions of A Midsummer Night's Dream

Rowe – Nicholas Rowe, *The Works of Mr William Shakespear* (1709)

Pope – Alexander Pope, *The Works of Shakespear* (1723)

Theobald – Lewis Theobald, *The Works of Shakespeare* (1733)

Hanmer – Thomas Hanmer, *The Works of Shakespear* (1744)

Halliwell – J. O. Halliwell, *The Complete Works of Shakespere revised* (1852)

Alexander – Peter Alexander, *William Shakespeare, The Complete Works* (1951)

Brooks – Harold F. Brooks, *A Midsummer Night's Dream* (Arden 2) (1979)

The only significant differences between the early printed texts that might be deemed worthy of additional comment come in the first and the last scenes:

- In both quarto texts, the stage direction for the entrance at 1.1.19 includes Helena in the list of characters. However, Helena does not speak in this scene, nor is she spoken to. It is possible that she is intended to be a silent presence (and some productions have chosen to have her appear but say nothing). However, it is also possible that Shakespeare originally intended her to be in this scene, putting her into the stage direction, but then changed his mind without deleting her from the entry. If F was printed in consultation with a prompt copy, it may reflect the fact that in the absence of any lines, Helena was not included in this entry on the early modern stage.

- In the two quarto texts, Philostrate, who is clearly Theseus's Master of the Revels, appears in Act 5, Scene 1 to provide Theseus with the list of entertainments proposed for his marriage celebrations. In the Folio text, Philostrate's lines are given to Egeus. This makes little sense, particularly with regards to Theseus's line: 'Where is our usual manager of mirth?' (5.1.35).

- In Q, Theseus reads out the list of entertainments himself, commenting on its contents occasionally as he goes. In F, however, Theseus, on receiving the paper of proposed entertainments, hands it to Lysander, and it is Lysander who reads out the names and descriptions of the proposed acts, with Theseus offering commentary on them in between. Harold F. Brooks suggests that 'The actors, like some editors, may have seen theatrical advantages in breaking up Theseus' longish speech.'[1] It is unclear whether such a revision was

---

1 Harold F. Brooks, ed., *A Midsummer Night's Dream*, Arden 2 edition (London: Methuen, 1979), 106.

authorial or theatrical and whether it became customary on the Elizabethan stage, but it has usually been followed in modern performances.

- Finally, the last speech of the scene is assigned in its entirety to Titania in the Folio text, with the lines from 'Now until the break of day' marked as a song.

VERSE AND PROSE IN THE PLAY

A Midsummer Night's Dream is reasonably traditional in its deployment of verse and prose. As one might expect, for most of the play the royal characters, lovers and fairies speak in verse, whilst the lower-class Mechanicals speak in prose.

However, this changes in the final scene of the play, where the Mechanicals' play is performed in verse. The intervening comments by the lovers and Theseus and Hippolyta are, contrastingly, in prose.

OTHER METRES

In addition to the iambic pentameter metre, in which most of the verse in the play is composed, Shakespeare uses other verse forms in the play, firstly for some of the dialogue of the magical characters (notably Puck, Oberon and the fairies), and secondly for elements of the play of 'Pyramus and Thisbe'.

The metre of 'Pyramus and Thisbe'

The play of 'Pyramus and Thisbe' is performed by the Mechanicals in Act 5, Scene 1. Prior to this we hear brief extracts from the play during the Mechanicals' rehearsal in Act 3, Scene 1. Here, Bottom's first speech is in iambic pentameter, with the rhyme pattern a b c b (heroic stanza).

> *Thisbe, the flowers of odorous savours sweet –*
> . . .
> *So hath thy breath, my dearest Thisbe dear.*
> *But hark, a voice! Stay thou but here awhile,*
> *And by and by I will to thee appear.*

(3.1.78–83)

However, after this, Flute's first four lines are alexandrines – lines of iambic hexameter (6 iambic feet/12 syllables in a line) with an alternate rhyme scheme.

> FLUTE   *Most radiant Pyramus, most lily-white of hue,*
> *Of colour like the red rose on triumphant briar,*
> *Most brisky juvenal, and eke most lovely Jew,*
> *As true as truest horse that yet would never tire;*

(3.1.89–92)

The alexandrine was less common in English than in French, although it had been used by poets of the sixteenth century, including Sir Philip Sidney.

When the play is eventually performed, it begins in a rather clunky iambic pentameter, with some awkward word order and 'words inserted to pad out the metre':[2]

> *This beauteous lady Thisbe is certain.*

(5.1.129)

Martin White asserts that Shakespeare is 'clearly mocking ... earlier styles of dramatic writing'.[3] The verse has an insistent

---

2   Martin White, *A Midsummer Night's Dream: A Guide to the Text and the Play in Performance* (Basingstoke: Palgrave Macmillan Ltd., 2008), 76.
3   Ibid., 76.

rhyming scheme (some alternate, some couplets), and many of the rhymes are comically forced:

> *And this the cranny is, right and sinister,*
> *Through which the fearful lovers are to whisper.*

(5.1.161–2)

The final speeches of Pyramus and Thisbe combine iambic pentameter with ballad metre – which alternates between iambic tetrameter (four feet per line – here divided into two) and iambic trimeter – (three feet per line) with a rhyme scheme: A(A) B C(C) B.

> *But stay! O spite!*
> *But mark, poor knight,*
> *What dreadful dole is here?*
> *Eyes, do you see?*
> *How can it be?*
> *O dainty duck! O dear!*

(5.1.265–70)

Again, with its excessive alliteration, this is a parody of some of the verse of the period. It is excessively sing-song in a way that seems inappropriate for the subject matter.

Magic metre

The magical figures in *A Midsummer Night's Dream* sometimes speak in iambic pentameter, but more often in other, shorter metres, the most common being trochaic tetrameter – four trochees (/ u) in a line.

The first time that we encounter a magical character – the Fairy – the first four lines are in anapaestic dimeter – two anapests – u u / in a line, with an alternate rhyme scheme:

FAIRY
   Over hill, over dale,
   u u   /   u u /
   Thorough bush, thorough brier,
   u   u   /   u   u   /
   Over park, over pale,
   Thorough flood, thorough fire,

                    (2.1.2–5)

The speech then moves into the more common rhyming couplets of tetrameter – mostly trochaic:

   Those be rubies, fairy favours,
   /   u / u   / u / u

                    (2.1.12)

with some iambic (u /) lines:

   To dew her orbs upon the green.
   u /   u /   u / u /

                    (2.1.9)

Most of the trochaic lines are catalectic (meaning that the last syllable is missing):

   I do wander everywhere,
   / u / u / u/

                    (2.1.6)

Catalectic trochaic tetrameter (with some lines of trochaic tetrameter and some of iambic tetrameter) is also the main metre used in 2.2 for Puck's speech (65–82); in 3.2 for Oberon's spell and his succeeding dialogue with Puck (102–21) and for Puck's rhymes (396–9 and 437–41); in 4.1 for the final lines spoken by Puck, Oberon and Titania (93–102); and in 5.1 for the final speeches of Puck, Oberon and Titania (357–424). A further occasional variation on this metrical line is a missing light beat at the caesura:

Up and down, up and down,
/   u   /   /   u   /

(3.2.396)

Yet but three? Come one more,

(3.2.437)

Trip away; make no stay;

(5.1.406)

A slightly more complex metrical form is used by Puck in 3.2 (448–63). The metre is, on the whole, trochaic; however, the lines are irregular in length, with a mixture of catalectic trochaic dimeter, catalectic trochaic tetrameter, iambic tetrameter and dimeter.

RHYME

A Midsummer Night's Dream contains a high proportion of rhyme. This takes the form both of rhyming couplets and alternating rhymes. Some rhyming couplets are found, as is common in Shakespeare's earlier work, at the ends of speeches and of scenes. The sense of the rhyme scheme is sometimes complicated by the fact that a pair of words which might have rhymed in Elizabethan pronunciation no longer rhyme today. It is the choice of the actor/ director whether to try to make the words rhyme, or to pronounce them as is common in modern English.

Two sets of characters in *A Midsummer Night's Dream* regularly speak in rhyme for long passages: the four lovers, Hermia, Helena, Lysander and Demetrius, and the magical characters, Oberon, Titania, Puck and the Fairy.

The lovers

In the first scene of the play the lovers begin by speaking blank verse, like their elders. However, once left alone in 1.1, as

Hermia and Lysander make their vow to meet in the wood they move into rhyming couplets (from line 171). Helena also takes up the form when she enters, with rhyme persisting until the end of the scene. Although Helena and Demetrius do not speak in rhyme on their first entrance into the wood in 2.1, from 2.2 onwards the lovers all speak in rhyme (a mixture of rhyming couplets and alternate rhyming lines) until the middle of 3.2 (lines 195–339) when they move back into blank verse for the more vicious section of their argument.

The use of rhyme produces an audible effect of artificiality, which may make these characters seem 'rather like puppets'.[4]

The fairies

The magical characters often speak in rhyme – either alternate rhymes or rhyming couplets – particularly when casting spells.

Titania uses rhyme least frequently, speaking in couplets only when charming Bottom in 3.1 and at the very start of 4.1 and when speaking in tetrameter at the end of 4.1 and end of 5.1. Titania and Oberon do not conduct their extended argument in 2.1 in rhyme.

IRREGULAR LINES

The verse of *A Midsummer Night's Dream* is quite regular, as one might expect from a play written in the mid–1590s. There are a few lines with a single missing syllable (here indicated by 'u'). A couple are headless lines (where there is a missing light beat before the first word), for example:

---

4 G. R. Hibbard, *The Making of Shakespeare's Dramatic Poetry* (Toronto: University of Toronto Press, 1981), 146.

u
That we are awake? It seems to me

(4.1.193)

There are also a couple of broken-backed lines, where the line is short by a single syllable, apparently at the mid-line caesura:

u
For parting us – O, is all forgot?

(3.2.201)

Finally, there are a few lines where an apparent one-syllable word might be drawn out to two syllables in length, for example at 2.1.58 ('But room, fairy! Here comes Oberon'). Brooks, in Arden 2, comments that 'Neither faëry ... nor any emendation for metre ... is wanted: the marshal-like cry of "room"! fills the place of a beat and a light syllable'.[5]

Short verse lines are relatively rare, partly due to the earliness of the play. There are a few lines that are short by between two and six syllables – 2.1.42, 3.1.103, 3.2.49, 3.2.100 and 5.1.71.

There are only two instances of more complex metrical irregularity:

- Out, loathèd medicine! O hated potion, hence!

  This line can be scanned as a line of regular length if 'medicine' is scanned as a two-syllable word ('med'cine') and ''d'cine O **hate**' treated as an anapest, or 'di-cine O **hate**' treated as a quartus paeon (see 'A Note on Metre'). Or it can be scanned as a hexameter – a line of six feet (see 'A Note on Metre')

5 Brooks, *A Midsummer Night's Dream*, 30.

- And what poor duty cannot do, noble respect

  Takes it in might, not merit. (5.1.91–2)

  Line 91 is 12 syllables in length and line 92 is made up of seven syllables. Theobald (1733) re-lineated, adding in the word 'willing' in order to regularize:

  > And what poor willing duty cannot do,
  >
  > Noble respect takes it in might, not merit.

  Brooks suggests that the short line at 92 is deliberate, closing 'the preceding movements of Theseus' speech, so that he can modulate into the key of his reminiscence'.[6]

PRONUNCIATION OF KEY WORDS

- The pronunciation of character names are given in the Dramatis Personae.
- Pronunciation of unusual names and places are given in the text.
- The word 'Athenian' is used regularly in the text – the metre suggests that it should sometimes be scanned as three syllables – A-**thee**-nian (as at 1.1.162) and sometimes as four syllables – A-**thee**-nee-**an** (as at 3.2.41).

YOU AND THOU IN THE PLAY

We may understand the difference between 'you' and 'thou' in Shakespeare as similar to that of 'vous' and 'tu' in French. 'You' (and its derivates: ye, your, etc.) is the plural and the more formal and polite form of address, whilst 'thou' (and its derivates: thee, thy, etc.) is more intimate and informal, marking a different type of relationship: one of superior to

---

6 Ibid., 109.

inferior, or lover to lover. Its informality may also make it appropriate in contexts where the speaker is being hateful, belittling or offensive.

Theseus and Hippolyta

Theseus uses 'thee' to Hippolyta, as we might expect, both as her betrothed and her conqueror. Her only use of a personal pronoun directed towards him is 'your' (5.1.209).

Lysander and Hermia

Lysander and Hermia converse mostly using the intimate 'thou' (with a few exceptions) in their intimate exchanges, and when Lysander rejects and abuses Hermia. However, following this rejection of Hermia in 3.2, she 'withdraws to [you] and never uses [thou] to him again'.[7]

Demetrius and Helena

Demetrius moves between 'thou' and 'you' with Helena, both when abusing her and when attempting intimacy. In return she mostly uses 'you', using 'thou' only three times in the play.[8]

Titania and Oberon

The first time that we see the fairy King and Queen in 2.1, they are using 'thou' to one another as a form of attack. Titania and Oberon use a mixture of 'you' and 'thou' to one another, both in argument and in intimate exchanges. Penelope Freedman notes that every time Oberon uses 'thou' to Titania 'she reciprocates, not to express affection, but because she recognises Oberon's uses as a strategy to dominate or manipulate her, and so replies in kind'.[9]

---

7 Penelope Freedman, *Power and Passion in Shakespeare's Pronouns: Interrogating 'you' and 'thou'* (Aldershot: Ashgate, 2007), 66.
8 Ibid., 67.
9 Ibid., 72.

Titania and Bottom

Titania, under the spell of the love potion, most commonly uses 'thou' to Bottom, whereas he uses 'you' to her, reflecting his confusion and his lack of investment in this unreciprocal relationship.

Hermia and Helena

In 1.1, Hermia uses 'thou' to Helena, but Helena uses 'you' to Hermia, resisting intimacy. Helena never uses 'thou' to Hermia in the whole play, whereas Hermia moves between the two forms.

For a more detailed discussion of the uses of pronouns in the play, see Penelope Freedman, *Power and Passion in Shakespeare's Pronouns*, 65–73.

KEY SOURCES

There is no specific source for the story of *A Midsummer Night's Dream*. However, as indicated in the notes, Shakespeare drew on a number of books when writing the play, the most notable being:

- Plutarch's *The Lives of the Noble Grecians and Romanes* (translated by Sir Thomas North, 1579), which supplied aspects of the life of Theseus.

  Plutarch has little to say of Hippolyta: 'Afterwards, at the end of four months, peace was taken between them by means of one of the women called Hippolyta. For this historiographer calleth the Amazon which Theseus married, Hippolyta, and not Antiopa.'[10]

10 Rev. Walter W. Skeat, *Shakespeare's Plutarch: Being a Selection from the Lives in North's Plutarch which Illustrate Shakespeare's Plays* (London: Macmillan and Company, 1875).

- Chaucer's *The Knight's Tale*, which supplies the story of Hippolyta's capture by Theseus in battle and their subsequent marriage:

Ther was a duc that highte Theseus;
Of Atthenes he was lord and governour,
And in his tyme swich a conquerour
That gretter was ther noon under the sonne.
Ful many a riche contree hadde he wonne;
What with his wysdom and his chivalrie,
He conquered al the regne of Femenye,
That whilom was ycleped Scithia,
And weddede the queene Ypolita,
And broghte hire hoom with hym in his contree
With muchel glorie and greet solemn[11]

In *The Knight's Tale* too the story of Theseus' wedding is interrupted by a story of love-rivalry, here that between Palamon and Arcite for the hand of Emilia. It is Shakespeare's provision of a second woman which allows *A Midsummer Night's Dream* to end as a comedy about two couples rather than a tragicomedy. (In collaboration with his younger colleague John Fletcher, Shakespeare would return to *The Knight's Tale* in his last play, *The Two Noble Kinsmen*, 1613: the wedding song for Theseus and Hipployta with which that play begins, 'Roses, their sharp spines being gone . . .', has sometimes been borrowed for transplantation into productions of *A Midsummer Night's Dream*.)

---

11 Larry D. Benson, ed., *The Riverside Chaucer* (Boston, MA: Houghton Mifflin, 1987), 37, lines 860–70.

- Ovid's *Metamorphoses* (translated by Arthur Golding, 1567, though Shakespeare also knew it in the original Latin) for the story of Pyramus and Thisbe, treated seriously in Ovid though other more parodic retellings of their fate pre-date *A Midsummer Night's Dream*. As elsewhere in the canon, Ovid provides Shakespeare's main source for his allusions to classical mythology in Daphne and Apollo, Philomel, Orpheus, and so on.

KEY FIGURES OF CLASSICAL MYTHOLOGY

Aeneas (A-**knee**-us) (1.1.174) – Greek/Roman myth. One of the Trojan leaders in the Trojan War. Fell in love with Dido, Queen of Carthage, but deserted her, after which she stabbed herself (source: Virgil, *Aeneid*).

Aurora (Or-**roar**-er) (3.2.380 and 3.2.389) – Roman myth. Goddess of the dawn.

Cadmus (4.1.112) – Greek myth. Founder and first king of Thebes.

centaurs (**Sen**-tors) (5.1.44) – Greek myth. Creatures half human, half horse.

Cephalus (**Ke**-full-**us**) (5.1.195-6) – Greek/Roman myth. Husband of Procris. Captured by Aurora he remained faithful to his wife (source: Ovid, *Metamorphoses*)

Cupid (1.1.235 and 2.1.157-165) – Roman myth. God of love and desire. Depicted with wings and sometimes as blind.

Diana (1.1.89) – Roman myth. Goddess of the hunt, the moon and chastity.

Dido (**Die**-do) (1.1.173) – Greek/Roman myth. Queen of Carthage. Fell in love with Aeneas. When Aeneas left she stabbed herself to death on a pyre (source: Virgil, *Aeneid*).

Dionysus (**Die**-on-**y**-sus) (5.1.48) – Greek myth. Also known as Bacchus. God of wine, madness, fertility and theatre. The followers of Dionysus were, known for their riotous, drunken behavior.

Fates (5.1.194, 5.1.273 and 5.1.322) – Greek and Roman myth. Three sister goddesses, thought to be responsible for man's destiny.

Furies (5.1.272) – Greek/Roman myth. Three godesses of justice and vengeance.

Hecate (**Heh**-kate) (5.1.369) – Greek myth. Goddess of sorcery and witchcraft.

Helen of Troy (5.1.11) – Greek myth. Known as the most beautiful woman in the world. Wife of King Menelaus of Sparta, she eloped with Paris, Prince of Troy. Her elopement initiated the Trojan War.

Hercules (**Her**-queue-**lees**) (1.2.25 and 4.1.112) – Roman myth. Son of Zeus. Famous for carrying out twelve Labours and for his strength and courage.

Hero (5.1.194) – Greek myth. Priestess of Aphrodite, dwelling on Sestos. Lover of Leander, who swam the Hellespont to be with her. She threw herself from a tower when she learnt of Leander's death.

Jove (5.1.175) – Roman myth. Otherwise known as Jupiter. King of the gods and god of sky and thunder.

Leander (5.1.193) – Greek myth. A young man from Abydos. In love with Hero. He would swim the Hellespont every night to be with her. He drowned one night in the rough waters.

Neptune (2.1.126 and 3.2.392) – Roman myth. God of the sea and fresh water.

Ninus (**Ny**-nus) (3.1.94 and 5.1.137) – Greek myth. Founder of Nineveh.

Orpheus (Or-**fay**-us) (5.1.49) – Greek myth. A musician and poet. According to some versions of Orpheus's story, he was killed by the Thracian Maenads, the worshippers of Dionysus, for not honouring their god.

Phoebe (**Fee**-bee) (1.1.209) – Greek myth. Goddess of the moon.

Phoebus (Phoebus Apollo) (**Fee**-bus A-**po**-llo) (1.2.31) – Greek myth. God of the light.

Philomel (**Fil**-o-**mel**) (2.2.13) – Greek myth. A princess of Athens. Having been raped and mutilated by her sister's husband, Tereus, she gained her revenge and was then transformed into a nightingale.

Procris (5.1.195-6) – Greek/Roman myth. Wife of Cephalus. Remained faithful when he tested her fidelity (source: Ovid, *Metamorphoses*).

Pyramus and Thisbe (1.2.12 and throughout) – two Babylonian lovers from adjoining houses, forbidden by their parents to be wed. Their story ends with both stabbing themselves to death. (source: Ovid, *Metamorphoses*).

Venus (3.2.61 and 107) – Roman myth. Goddess of love. Planet in the solar system.

SUGGESTED FURTHER READING

For further detailed information about the play, we refer the reader to the Arden 2 edition, which contains material on the text(s), sources, critical history and performance history:

Brooks, Harold F. *A Midsummer Night's Dream*. Arden 2 edition. London: Methuen, 1979.

Freedman, Penelope. *Power and Passion in Shakespeare's Pronouns: Interrogating 'you' and 'thou'*. Aldershot: Ashgate, 2007.

Griffiths, Trevor R., ed. *A Midsummer Night's Dream (Shakespeare in Production)*. Cambridge: Cambridge University Press, 1996.

Halio, Jay. *A Midsummer Night's Dream: Shakespeare in Performance*, 2nd edition. Manchester: Manchester University Press, 2012.

Rokison, Abigail. *Shakespearean Verse Speaking: Text and Theatre Practice*. Cambridge: Cambridge University Press, 2010.

Wright, George T. *Shakespeare's Metrical Art*. London: University of California Press, 1988.

DRAMATIS PERSONAE

THESEUS, Duke of Athens – Pron. either **Thee**-seus (as at 1.1.20)
   (equiv. 2 syl.) or **Thee**-see-**us** (as at 2.1.76) (equiv. 3 syl.).

HIPPOLYTA, Queen of the Amazons, betrothed to Theseus – Pron.
   Hi-**pol**-i-**ta**.

PHILOSTRATE, Master of the Revels to Theseus – Pron.
   Phil-oh-**straight**.

EGEUS, Father to Hermia – Pron. Eh-**gee**-us.

HERMIA, Athenian lady, Daughter to Egeus – Pron. either **Her**-
   mia (as at 1.1.46) (equiv. 2 syl.) or **Her**-mee-**a** (as at 1.1.23)
   (equiv. 3 syl.).

DEMETRIUS, Athenian man – Pron. either Dem-**ee**-trius (as at 1.1.52)
   (equiv. 3 syl.) or Dem-**ee**-tree-**us** (as at 1.1.24) (equiv. 4 syl.).

LYSANDER, Athenian man – Pron. Lie-**san**-der.

HELENA, Athenian lady – Pron. either **Hel**-na (as at 1.1.200)
   (equiv. 2 syl. – though more often changed to Helen when the
   metre permits only 2 syllables) or **Hel**-en-**a** (as at 1.1.180)
   (equiv. 3 syl.).

QUINCE, a Carpenter.

BOTTOM, a Weaver.

FLUTE, a Bellows-mender.

STARVELING, a Tailor.

SNOUT, a Tinker.

SNUG, a Joiner.

PUCK, or Robin Goodfellow, a sprite.

FAIRY (in 2.1 – possibly one of the four named Fairies).

OBERON, King of the Fairies – Pron. **O**-ber-**on**.

TITANIA, Queen of the Fairies – Pron. either Tit-**ah**-nia (as at
   2.1.119) (equiv. 3 syl.) or Tit-**ah**-ni-**a** (as at 2.1.60).

PEASE-BLOSSOM, a Fairy.

COBWEB, a Fairy.

MOTH, a Fairy.

MUSTARD-SEED, a Fairy.

Additional Fairies.

A MIDSUMMER
NIGHT'S DREAM

ACT 1, SCENE 1

Enter THESEUS, HIPPOLYTA, *and [*PHILOSTRATE]
with Attendants

THESEUS
    Now, fair Hippolyta, our nuptial hour
    Draws on apace; four happy days bring in
    Another moon: but O, methinks, how slow
    This old moon wanes! She lingers my desires,
    Like to a step-dame or a dowager   5
    Long withering out a young man's revenue.

HIPPOLYTA
    Four days will quickly steep themselves in night;
    Four nights will quickly dream away the time;
    And then the moon, like to a silver bow
    New-bent in heaven, shall behold the night   10
    Of our solemnities.

THESEUS   Go Philostrate,
    Stir up the Athenian youth to merriments;
    Awake the pert and nimble spirit of mirth;
    Turn melancholy forth to funerals;
    The pale companion is not for our pomp.   15

[Exit PHILOSTRATE]

    Hippolyta, I woo'd thee with my sword,
    And won thy love doing thee injuries;
    But I will wed thee in another key,
    With pomp, with triumph, and with reveling.

nuptial hour – *wedding*
apace – *quickly*

lingers – *delays fulfilment of*
like to – *like*; step-dame – *stepmother*; dowager – *widow*
withering out – *delaying*; revenue – *inheritance*   **with**-ering (equiv. 2 syl.)

steep – *bathe*   Q1 – night Q2/F – nights

like to – *like*

                                                                 Rowe – New-bent Qq/F – Now bent
solemnities – *celebrations*

                                                                 the Ath-**e**-nian (equiv. 3 syl.)
pert – *swift*; mirth – *happiness*   spirit (equiv.1 syl.)

not for our pomp – *not welcome at our celebration*   com-**pan**-ion (equiv. 3 syl.)

    Source: Chaucer, *The Knight's Tale* – Hippolyta was captured by Theseus in battle
injuries – *wrongs*
key – *mood*
triumph – *public rejoicing*

Enter EGEUS *and his daughter* HERMIA, LYSANDER *and*
DEMETRIUS

EGEUS

Happy be Theseus, our renownèd Duke!   20

THESEUS

Thanks, good Egeus. What's the news with thee?

EGEUS

Full of vexation come I, with complaint
Against my child, my daughter Hermia.
Stand forth Demetrius. My noble lord,
This man hath my consent to marry her.   25
Stand forth Lysander. And, my gracious duke,
This hath bewitch'd the bosom of my child.
Thou, thou Lysander, thou hast given her rhymes,
And interchang'd love-tokens with my child:
Thou hast by moonlight at her window sung   30
With faining voice verses of feigning love,
And stol'n the impression of her fantasy
With bracelets of thy hair, rings, gawds, conceits,
Knacks, trifles, nosegays, sweetmeats (messengers
Of strong prevailment in unharden'd youth):   35
With cunning hast thou filch'd my daughter's heart,
Turn'd her obedience (which is due to me)
To stubborn harshness. And, my gracious Duke,
Be it so she will not here, before your Grace,
Consent to marry with Demetrius,   40
I beg the ancient privilege of Athens:
As she is mine, I may dispose of her;
Which shall be either to this gentleman,
Or to her death, according to our law
Immediately provided in that case.   45

Qq SDs have Helena enter here as well, but she does not speak

bosom – *heart*

rhymes – *poems*

F2 – This Qq/F – This man

given (equiv.1 syl.)

faining – *soft*; feigning – *deceitful*

stol'n . . . fantasy – *imprinted yourself on her imagination*   stol'n (equiv. 1 syl.)

gawds – *showy toys*; conceits – *trinkets*

knacks – *knick-knacks*; nosegays – *posies*

prevailment – *influence*; unharden'd – *inexperienced*

filch'd – *stolen*

ob-**e**-dience (equiv.3 syl.)

Be it – *If it is*   Be it **so** (anapest – see 'A Note on Metre')

privilege – *right*

Immediately – *expressly*   Imm-**e**-diate-**ly** (equiv. 4 syl.)

THESEUS
    What say you, Hermia? Be advised, fair maid.
    To you your father should be as a god:
    One that compos'd your beauties, yea, and one
    To whom you are but as a form in wax
    By him imprinted, and within his power   50
    To leave the figure, or disfigure it.
    Demetrius is a worthy gentleman.

HERMIA
    So is Lysander.

THESEUS   In himself he is;
    But in this kind, wanting your father's voice,
    The other must be held the worthier.   55

HERMIA
    I would my father look'd but with my eyes.

THESEUS
    Rather your eyes must with his judgment look.

HERMIA
    I do entreat your Grace to pardon me.
    I know not by what power I am made bold,
    Nor how it may concern my modesty   60
    In such a presence here to plead my thoughts,
    But I beseech your Grace that I may know
    The worst that may befall me in this case,
    If I refuse to wed Demetrius.

THESEUS
    Either to die the death, or to abjure   65
    For ever the society of men.

as a – *like a*
compos'd – *fashioned*
as a form . . . imprinted – *like a wax impression of his seal*

leave – *maintain*; disfigure – *destroy/ mar*

kind – *respect*; wanting – *lacking*; voice – *vote*

would – *wish*

power (equiv.1 syl.)

concern – *suit with*
such a presence – *present company/ such a place*

know . . . worst – Prov.

befall me – *happen to me*

die the death – *be put to death*; abjure – *renounce/ reject*
society – *company*

Therefore, fair Hermia, question your desires,
Know of your youth, examine well your blood,
Whether, if you yield not to your father's choice,
You can endure the livery of a nun,   70
For aye to be in shady cloister mew'd,
To live a barren sister all your life,
Chanting faint hymns to the cold fruitless moon.
Thrice blessèd they that master so their blood
To undergo such maiden pilgrimage;   75
But earthlier happy is the rose distill'd,
Than that which withering on the virgin thorn,
Grows, lives and dies in single blessedness.

HERMIA

So will I grow, so live, so die, my lord,
Ere I will yield my virgin patent up   80
Unto his lordship whose unwishèd yoke
My soul consents not to give sovereignty.

THESEUS

Take time to pause; and by the next new moon,
The sealing-day betwixt my love and me
For everlasting bond of fellowship,   85
Upon that day either prepare to die
For disobedience to your father's will,
Or else to wed Demetrius, as he would,
Or on Diana's altar to protest,
For aye, austerity and single life.   90

DEMETRIUS

Relent, sweet Hermia; and Lysander, yield
Thy crazéd title to my certain right.

Know of – *inquire of*; blood – *passions*

Whether (equiv.1 syl.)

livery – *habit*   **liv**-ery (equiv. 2 syl.)

aye – *always*; mew'd – *cooped up*

fruitless – *barren*

master – *control*; blood – *passions*

maiden pilgrimage – *life as a virgin*

earthlier happy – *more happy on earth*; distll'd – *(for perfume)*   **earth**-lier (equiv. 2 syl.)

with-ering (equiv. 2 syl.)

single blessedness – *celibacy*

Ere – *Before*; virgin patent – *entitlement to virginity*

his lordship – *a husband/ Demetrius*; unwishèd yoke – *dominion*

sovereignty – *rule*   **sov**-ereign-**ty** (equiv. 3 syl.)

sealing-day – *wedding day*

dis-ob-**e**-dience (equiv. 4 syl.)

he would – *your father wishes*

Diana – (see Myth); protest – *vow*

aye – *ever*; austerity – *self-denial*

crazéd title – *mad/flawed claim*; certain – *definite*

LYSANDER

You have her father's love Demetrius:
Let me have Hermia's; do you marry him.

EGEUS

Scornful Lysander, true, he hath my love;   95
And what is mine my love shall render him;
And she is mine, and all my right of her
I do estate unto Demetrius.

LYSANDER

I am, my lord, as well deriv'd as he,
As well possess'd; my love is more than his;   100
My fortunes every way as fairly rank'd,
If not with vantage, as Demetrius';
And, which is more than all these boasts can be,
I am belov'd of beauteous Hermia.
Why should not I then prosecute my right?   105
Demetrius, I'll avouch it to his head,
Made love to Nedar's daughter, Helena,
And won her soul: and she, sweet lady, dotes,
Devoutly dotes, dotes in idolatry,
Upon this spotted and inconstant man.   110

THESEUS

I must confess that I have heard so much,
And with Demetrius thought to have spoke thereof;
But being over-full of self-affairs,
My mind did lose it. But, Demetrius, come,
And come, Egeus; you shall go with me: 115
I have some private schooling for you both.
For you, fair Hermia, look you arm yourself
To fit your fancies to your father's will;
Or else the law of Athens yields you up

do you – *why don't you*

render – *give to*
right of – *claim to*
estate unto – *bestow upon*

well deriv'd – *of as good family*
well possess'd – *affluent*
fairly – *equally*
with vantage ... Demetrius – *exceeding those of Demetrius*
which – *what*
belov'd of – *loved by*   **beau**-teous (equiv. 2 syl.)
prosecute – *pursue*
avouch it – *declare*; head – *face*
Made love to – *courted*   Nedar – Pron. – **Nay**-dar
dotes – *is infatuated with*
in idolatry – *with admiration*
spotted and inconstant – *stained with fickleness*

to have **spoke** (anapest – see 'A Note on Metre')
over-full ... affairs – *overly occupied with my own concerns*
lose – *forget about*

schooling – *advice*
arm – *prepare*
fancies – *desires*
yields you up – *gives you*

(Which by no means we may extenuate)   120
To death, or to a vow of single life.
Come, my Hippolyta; what cheer, my love?
Demetrius and Egeus, go along;
I must employ you in some business
Against our nuptial, and confer with you   125
Of something nearly that concerns yourselves.

EGEUS
With duty and desire we follow you.

Exeunt all but LYSANDER *and* HERMIA

LYSANDER
How now, my love? Why is your cheek so pale?
How chance the roses there do fade so fast?

HERMIA
Belike for want of rain, which I could well   130
Beteem them from the tempest of my eyes.

LYSANDER
Ay me! For aught that I could ever read,
Could ever hear by tale or history,
The course of true love never did run smooth;
But either it was different in blood –   135

HERMIA
O cross! too high to be enthrall'd to low.

LYSANDER
Or else misgraffèd in respect of years –

extenuate – *mitigate*

what cheer – *what's the matter*
go – *come*

bus-i-**ness** (equiv. 3 syl.)

Against – *In preparation for*
nearly that – *that closely*

Lysander begins with the formal address – 'you' but then moves to the intimate
chance – *comes it*   'thou'/ 'thee' (161)

Belike – *probably*
Beteem – *allow*   Qq – my eyes F – mine eyes

aught – *anything*   Qq – I could ever read F – ever I could read

in blood – *in rank/class*   **diff**-er-**ent** (equiv. 3 syl.)

cross – *vexation*   Theobald – low Qq/F – love

misgrafféd – *ill matched*

HERMIA

O spite! too old to be engag'd to young.

LYSANDER

Or else it stood upon the choice of friends –

HERMIA

O hell! to choose love by another's eyes.   140

LYSANDER

Or if there were a sympathy in choice,
War, death, or sickness did lay siege to it,
Making it momentany as a sound,
Swift as a shadow, short as any dream,
Brief as the lightning in the collied night,   145
That, in a spleen, unfolds both heaven and earth,
And, ere a man hath power to say 'Behold!',
The jaws of darkness do devour it up:
So quick bright things come to confusion.

HERMIA

If then true lovers have been ever cross'd,   150
It stands as an edict in destiny.
Then let us teach our trial patience,
Because it is a customary cross,
As due to love as thoughts and dreams and sighs,
Wishes and tears, poor fancy's followers.   155

LYSANDER

A good persuasion; therefore hear me, Hermia.
I have a widow aunt, a dowager
Of great revenue, and she hath no child –
From Athens is her house remote seven leagues –
And she respects me as her only son.   160

stood – *was dependent*; friends – *kin*   Qq – friends F – merit

                                                            Qq – eyes F – eye

sympathy – *agreement*

momentany – *momentary*   Qq – momentany F – momentarie

collied – *coal black*
spleen – *fit of passion*; unfolds – *reveals*   heaven (equiv. 1 syl.)

quick – *quickly (adv.)/lively (adj.)*   con-**fu**-si-**on** (equiv. 4 syl.)

ever cross'd – *always vexed*
an edict in destiny – *an official proclamation of destiny*
                                    tri-al (equiv. 2 syl.); **pat**-i-**ence** (equiv. 3 syl.)

due – *suited*
fancy's – *love's*

A good persuasion – *well urged*
dowager – *a widow with a title derived from her late husband*
revenue – *income* revenue – Pron. – metre suggests emphasis on 2nd syl. – re-**ven**-ue
                                              Qq – remote F – remov'd
respects – *regards*

There gentle Hermia, may I marry thee,
And to that place the sharp Athenian law
Cannot pursue us. If thou lov'st me then,
Steal forth thy father's house tomorrow night;
And in the wood, a league without the town   165
(Where I did meet thee once with Helena
To do observance to a morn of May),
There will I stay for thee.

HERMIA   My good Lysander,
I swear to thee by Cupid's strongest bow,
By his best arrow with the golden head,   170
By the simplicity of Venus' doves,
By that which knitteth souls and prospers loves,
And by that fire which burn'd the Carthage queen
When the false Trojan under sail was seen;
By all the vows that ever men have broke   175
(In number more than ever women spoke),
In that same place thou hast appointed me,
Tomorrow truly will I meet with thee.

LYSANDER
Keep promise, love. Look, here comes Helena.

Enter HELENA.

HERMIA
God speed fair Helena! Whither away?   180

HELENA
Call you me fair? That fair again unsay!
Demetrius loves your fair: O happy fair!
Your eyes are lode-stars, and your tongue's sweet air

forth – *away from*
without – *outside*

do observance to a morn of May – *celebrate May Day*   Qq – to a F – for a
stay – *wait*

arrow ... head – *the arrow said to create love*
simplicity – *innocence*   Rhyme – from 1.171 the lovers speak mainly in couplets
knitteth – *knits together*; prospers – *makes flourish*   Q1 – loves F/Q2 – love
that fire – *Dido's funeral pyre*; the Carthage queen – *Dido, Queen of Carthage* (see Myth)
the false Trojan – *Aeneas*   Source: The story of Dido and Aeneas in Virgil's *Aeneid*

appointed me – *told me to come*

Whither away – *where are you going?*

happy fair – *fortunate beauty*
lode-stars – *guiding stars*; air – *melody*

More tuneable than lark to shepherd's ear,
When wheat is green, when hawthorn buds appear.   185
Sickness is catching; O were favour so,
Yours would I catch, fair Hermia, ere I go:
My ear should catch your voice, my eye your eye,
My tongue should catch your tongue's sweet melody.
Were the world mine, Demetrius being bated,   190
The rest I'd give to be to you translated.
O, teach me how you look, and with what art
You sway the motion of Demetrius' heart.

HERMIA
I frown upon him; yet he loves me still.

HELENA
O that your frowns would teach my smiles such skill!   195

HERMIA
I give him curses; yet he gives me love.

HELENA
O that my prayers could such affection move!

HERMIA
The more I hate, the more he follows me.

HELENA
The more I love, the more he hateth me.

HERMIA
His folly, Helena, is no fault of mine.   200

HELENA
None but your beauty; would that fault were mine!

tuneable – *melodious*

favour – *good looks/charm*

          Hanmer – Yours would I Qq/F – Your words I F2 – Your words Ide

bated – *excepted*

to you translated – *transformed into you*   Hanmer – I'd Qq/F – Ile

art – *skill/magic*

motion – *desire*

Q1 – no fault Q2/F – none

would – *if only*

HERMIA

    Take comfort: he no more shall see my face;
    Lysander and myself will fly this place.
    Before the time I did Lysander see,
    Seem'd Athens as a paradise to me. 205
    O then what graces in my love do dwell,
    That he hath turn'd a heaven unto a hell!

LYSANDER

    Helen, to you our minds we will unfold:
    Tomorrow night, when Phoebe doth behold
    Her silver visage in the wat'ry glass, 210
    Decking with liquid pearl the bladed grass
    (A time that lovers' flights doth still conceal),
    Through Athens' gates have we devis'd to steal.

HERMIA

    And in the wood, where often you and I
    Upon faint primrose beds were wont to lie, 215
    Emptying our bosoms of their counsel sweet,
    There my Lysander and myself shall meet;
    And thence from Athens turn away our eyes,
    To seek new friends, and stranger companies.
    Farewell, sweet playfellow; pray thou for us, 220
    And good luck grant thee thy Demetrius!
    Keep word, Lysander; we must starve our sight
    From lovers' food, till morrow deep midnight.

Exit Hermia.

LYSANDER

    I will my Hermia. Helena, adieu;
    As you on him, Demetrius dote on you! 225

Q1 – as Q2/F – like

graces in my love – *charms in Lysander*

heaven (equiv. 1 syl.); Q1 – unto Q2/F – into

Phoebe – *the moon* (see Myth)   Phoebe – Pron. – **Fee**-bee

visage – *face*; wat'ry glass – *body of water*

liquid pearl – *dew*

still – *always*

faint – *pale*; wont – *accustomed*

counsel – *secrets*   **Emp**-tying (equiv. 2 syl.)

stranger companies – *the company of strangers*

morrow – *tomorrow*

[Exit Lysander]

HELENA

How happy some o'er other some can be!
Through Athens I am thought as fair as she.
But what of that? Demetrius thinks not so;
He will not know what all but he do know:
And as he errs, doting on Hermia's eyes,   230
So I, admiring of his qualities:
Things base and vile, holding no quantity,
Love can transpose to form and dignity:
Love looks not with the eyes, but with the mind;
And therefore is wing'd Cupid painted blind: 235
Nor hath Love's mind of any judgement taste;
Wings and no eyes figure unheedy haste:
And therefore is Love said to be a child,
Because in choice he is so oft beguil'd.
As waggish boys in game themselves forswear,   240
So the boy Love is perjur'd every where:
For ere Demetrius look'd on Hermia's eyne,
He hail'd down oaths that he was only mine;
And when this hail some heat from Hermia felt,
So he dissolv'd, and show'rs of oaths did melt.   245
I will go tell him of fair Hermia's flight:
Then to the wood will he to-morrow night
Pursue her; and for this intelligence
If I have thanks, it is a dear expense:
But herein mean I to enrich my pain,   250
To have his sight thither and back again.

Exit

some o'er other some – *some more than others*

Qq – do F – doth

errs – *mistakes*

holding no quanity – *bearing no value*
transpose to – *turn into*; form – *attractive appearance*

And . . . blind – *(Cupid was depicted as a child with wings and a blindfold)* (see Myth)
of . . . taste – *any reason*
figure – *symbolize*

beguil'd – *deceived*   Q1 – is so oft F2 – often is
waggish – *mischievous*; game – *jest*; themselves forswear – *break their word*

ere – *before*; eyne – *eyes*

dissolv'd – *broke faith/melted*

intelligence – *information*   Qq – this F – his
dear expense – *costly (to her and Demetrius)/worth the effort*
enrich my pain – *enrich myself by my pains*
thither – *there*

ACT 1, SCENE 2

Enter QUINCE, SNUG, BOTTOM, FLUTE, SNOUT,
and STARVELING

QUINCE
Is all our company here?

BOTTOM
You were best to call them generally, man by man,
according to the scrip.

QUINCE
Here is the scroll of every man's name which is
thought fit through all Athens to play in our   5
interlude before the Duke and the Duchess, on his
wedding-day at night.

BOTTOM
First, good Peter Quince, say what the play treats
on; then read the names of the actors; and so grow
to a point.   10

QUINCE
Marry, our play is 'The most lamentable comedy,
and most cruel death of Pyramus and Thisbe'.

BOTTOM
A very good piece of work, I assure you, and a
merry. Now, good Peter Quince, call forth your
actors by the scroll. Masters, spread yourselves.   15

QUINCE
Answer as I call you. Nick Bottom, the weaver.

The Mechanicals' scene is in PROSE

generally – *(malapropism for severally)*
scrip – *script*

interlude – *play*

treats on – *is about*
grow ... point – *draw to a conclusion*

Qq – to F – on to

Source: The story of Pyramus and Thisbe, Ovid's *Metamorphosis* (see Myth)

spread yourselves – *spread out*

BOTTOM
Ready. Name what part I am for, and proceed.

QUINCE
You, Nick Bottom, are set down for Pyramus.

BOTTOM
What is Pyramus? A lover, or a tyrant?

QUINCE
A lover, that kills himself most gallant for love.   20

BOTTOM
That will ask some tears in the true performing of it.
If I do it, let the audience look to their eyes: I will
move storms, I will condole in some measure. To the
rest – yet my chief humour is for a tyrant: I could
play Ercles rarely, or a part to tear a cat in, to make   25
all split.
  The raging rocks,
  And shivering shocks,
  Shall break the locks
  Of prison gates;   30
  And Phibbus' car
  Shall shine from far
  And make and mar
  The foolish fates.
This was lofty! Now name the rest of the players.   35
This is Ercles' vein, a tyrant's vein: a lover is
more condoling.

QUINCE
Francis Flute, the bellows-mender.

Qq – gallant F – gallantly

ask – *require*
look to their eyes – *try not to cry*
condole – *lament*
humour – *inclination*
Ercles – *Hercules* (see Myth); rarely – *exceptionally*; tear a cat in – *rant and rave*
split – *go to pieces*
        Metre – This recitation is in iambic dimeter (two iambic feet in the line)
shivering – *shattering*   **shiv**-ering (equiv. 2 syl.)

Phibbus' car – *the chariot of Phoebus Apollo, the sun god* (see Myth)

make and mar – *make and break*
fates – *the three classical goddesses of destiny*
lofty – *sublime*
Ercles' vein – *the temperament of Hercules*
condoling – *sympathetic*

FLUTE

    Here, Peter Quince.

QUINCE

    Flute, you must take Thisbe on you.   40

FLUTE

    What is Thisbe? A wandering knight?

QUINCE

    It is the lady that Pyramus must love.

FLUTE

    Nay, faith, let me not play a woman: I have a beard
    coming.

QUINCE

    That's all one: you shall play it in a mask; and   45
    you may speak as small as you will.

BOTTOM

    An I may hide my face, let me play Thisbe too. I'll
    speak in a monstrous little voice: 'Thisne,
    Thisne!' – 'Ah, Pyramus, lover dear! thy Thisbe dear,
    and lady dear!'   50

QUINCE

    No, no, you must play Pyramus; and Flute, you
    Thisbe.

BOTTOM

    Well, proceed.

mask – *(possibly a full face mask, but more likely the usual outdoor masks worn by*
small – *high* *Elizabethan women)*

An – *If*
monstrous – *extraordinarily*; Thisne – *pet-name for Thisbe*

QUINCE

Robin Starveling, the tailor?

STARVELING

Here, Peter Quince.   55

QUINCE

Robin Starveling, you must play Thisbe's mother.
Tom Snout, the tinker?

SNOUT

Here, Peter Quince.

QUINCE

You, Pyramus' father; my selfe, Thisbe's father;
Snug, the joiner, you the lion's part. And I hope here   60
is a play fitted.

SNUG

Have you the lion's part written? Pray you, if it
be, give it me; for I am slow of study.

QUINCE

You may do it extempore, for it is nothing but
roaring.   65

BOTTOM

Let me play the lion too. I will roar, that I will
do any man's heart good to hear me. I will roar, that
I will make the Duke say: 'Let him roar again: let him
roar again'.

QUINCE

And you should do it too terribly, you would fright   70

Qq – here F – there

fitted – *well equipped*

do it extempore – *improvise it*

And – *If*, terribly – *horrifyingly*

Q1 – And Q2/F – If

the Duchess and the ladies, that they would shriek: and
that were enough to hang us all.

ALL

That would hang us, every mother's son.

BOTTOM

I grant you, friends, if you should fright the ladies
out of their wits, they would have no more discretion   75
but to hang us. But I will aggravate my voice so, that
I will roar you as gently as any sucking dove; I will
roar you and 'twere any nightingale.

QUINCE

You can play no part but Pyramus: for Pyramus is a
sweet-faced man; a proper man as one shall see in a   80
summer's day; a most lovely, gentleman-like man:
therefore you must needs play Pyramus.

BOTTOM

Well, I will undertake it. What beard were I best
to play it in?

QUINCE

Why, what you will.   85

BOTTOM

I wil discharge it in either your straw-colour beard,
your orange-tawny beard, your purple-in-grain
beard, or your French crown colour beard, your
perfect yellow.

every mother's son – Prov.

Qq – if F – if that

discretion – *sound judgement*
aggravate – *intensify (malapropism for mitigate or moderate)*
sucking dove – *(confusing the sitting dove and sucking lamb)*   Qq – roar you F – roar
and 'twere – *as though it were*

proper – *handsome*   proper ... day – Prov.

discharge – *perform*
orange-tawny – *tan-coloured*; purple-in-grain – *red*
French crown – *a gold coin*   Qq – colour F – colour'd

QUINCE

Some of your French crowns have no hair at all,   90
and then you will play bare-faced. But, masters,
here are your parts; and I am to entreat you, request
you, and desire you, to con them by tomorrow
night; and meet me in the palace wood, a mile without
the town, by moonlight; there will we rehearse,   95
for if we meet in the city, we shall be dogg'd with
company, and our devices known. In the meantime
I will draw a bill of properties, such as our play
wants. I pray you fail me not.

BOTTOM

We will meet, and there we may rehearse most   100
obscenely and courageously. Take pains, be perfect:
adieu!

QUINCE

At the Duke's oak we meet.

BOTTOM

Enough: hold, or cut bow-strings.

Exeunt.

ACT 2, SCENE 1

Enter a Fairy at one door, and Puck at another.

PUCK

How now, spirit! Whither wander you?

FAIRY

Over hill, over dale,

Some ... at all – *(being bald from 'French-disease' – syphilis)*
bare-faced – *beardless/undiguised*

con – *learn*

                                                  Qq – will we Q2/F – we will

dogg'd with – *plagued with*
devices – *plans*
draw – *draw up*; bill – *list*

obscenely – *(malapropism for seemly)*; perfect – *word perfect*

hold ... bow-strings – *(Prov. from archery – the meaning is unsure but the sense is
'keep your word or be shamed')*

Whither – *Where*   Metre – this line is headless (see 'A Note on Metre')

Metre – the speech begins in anapaestic dimeter – see Introduction – Magic Metre.
                                Rhyme – alternate rhyming lines

Thorough bush, thorough brier,
Over park, over pale,
Thorough flood, thorough fire, 5
I do wander everywhere,
Swifter than the moon's sphere;
And I serve the Fairy Queen,
To dew her orbs upon the green.
The cowslips tall her pensioners be, 10
In their gold coats spots you see;
Those be rubies, fairy favours,
In those freckles live their savours.
I must go seek some dew-drops here,
And hang a pearl in every cowslip's ear. 15
Farewell, thou lob of spirits; I'll be gone;
Our Queen and all her elves come here anon.

PUCK
The King doth keep his revels here tonight;
Take heed the Queen come not within his sight;
For Oberon is passing fell and wrath, 20
Because that she as her attendant hath
A lovely boy, stol'n, from an Indian king –
She never had so sweet a changeling;
And jealous Oberon would have the child
Knight of his train, to trace the forests wild: 25
But she perforce withholds the lovèd boy,
Crowns him with flowers, and makes him all her joy.
And now they never meet in grove or green,
By fountain clear, or spangled starlight sheen,
But they do square; that all their elves for fear 30
Creep into acorn-cups, and hide them there.

Thorough – *through*   Q1 – Thorough Q2/F – Through
pale – *enclosure*

                                                             Q1 – Thorough Q2/F – Through
Metre – speech moves into rhyming tetrameter couplets (see Intro. – Magic Metre)
sphere – *the transparent globe thought to carry*   **moo**-n's (equiv. 2 syl.)
the moon around the earth
orbs – *circles/fairy rings*
pensioners – *bodyguards*   **pen**-sioners (equiv. 2 syl.)
In ... rubies – *(cowslips contain small red spots)*
favours – *marks of favour*
savours – *scent*

                              Metre – the speech moves into iambic pentameter
lob – *country lout*
anon – *soon*

keep – *hold*

passing ... wrath – *extremely fierce and angry*

                                        stol'n (equiv. 1 syl.); F – stol'n Q – stolen
changeling – *mortal child stolen by fairies*   **chan**-ge-**ling** (equiv. 3 syl.)

of his train – *in his retinue*; trace – *range*
perforce – *forcibly*

sheen – *shining*
square – *quarrel*

FAIRY

    Either I mistake your shape and making quite,
    Or else you are that shrewd and knavish sprite
    Call'd Robin Goodfellow. Are not you he
    That frights the maidens of the villagery,   35
    Skim milk, and sometimes labour in the quern,
    And bootless make the breathless housewife churn,
    And sometime make the drink to beare no barm,
    Mislead night-wanderers, laughing at their harm?
    Those that Hobgoblin call you, and sweet Puck,   40
    You do their work, and they shall have good luck.
    Are not you he?

PUCK   Thou speak'st aright;
    I am that merry wanderer of the night.
    I jest to Oberon, and make him smile
    When I a fat and bean-fed horse beguile,   45
    Neighing in likeness of a filly foal;
    And sometime lurk I in a gossip's bowl
    In very likeness of a roasted crab,
    And when she drinks, against her lips I bob,
    And on her wither'd dewlap pour the ale.   50
    The wisest aunt, telling the saddest tale,
    Sometime for three-foot stool mistaketh me;
    Then slip I from her bum, down topples she,
    And 'tailor' cries, and falls into a cough;
    And then the whole quire hold their hips and loffe   55
    And waxen in their mirth, and neeze, and swear
    A merrier hour was never wasted there.
    But room, fairy! Here comes Oberon.

FAIRY

    And here my mistress. Would that he were gone!

making – *build*

Ei-ther **I** (anapest – see 'A Note on Metre')

shrewd – *mischievous*

Q1 – not you Q2/F – you not

villagery – *village*

vill-a-**gery** (equiv. 3 syl.)

Skim – *take the cream off*; quern – *mill*

bootless – *in vain*

the drink – *ale*; barm – *yeast/ frothy head*

wan-derers (equiv. 2 syl.)

Metre – This line is short by 2 syl.

wan-derer (equiv. 2 syl.)

jest – *play the jester*

bean-fed – *well fed*; beguile – *trick*

filly foal – *female foal*

gossip's – *a tattling woman's*

crab – *crab apple*

bob – *knock*

dewlap – *folds of flesh around the throat*

aunt – *old woman*

'tailor' – *(cry of shock – possibly because she falls on her 'tail')*

quire – *company*; loffe – *laugh*

waxen – *increase*; neeze – *sneeze*

merr-ier (equiv. 2 syl.)

room – *make room*

ro-om (equiv. 2 syl.) (see Introduction)

Would that – *If only*

Enter OBERON, *the King of Fairies, at one door, with his train;*
and TITANIA, *the Queen, at another, with hers.*

OBERON

Ill met by moonlight, proud Titania.   60

TITANIA

What, jealous Oberon? Fairies, skip hence;
I have forsworn his bed and company.

OBERON

Tarry, rash wanton; am not I thy lord?

TITANIA

Then I must be thy lady; but I know
When thou hast stol'n away from fairy land,   65
And in the shape of Corin, sat all day
Playing on pipes of corn, and versing love
To amorous Phillida. Why art thou here,
Come from the farthest step of India,
But that, forsooth, the bouncing Amazon,   70
Your buskin'd mistress and your warrior love,
To Theseus must be wedded, and you come
To give their bed joy and prosperity?

OBERON

How canst thou thus, for shame, Titania,
Glance at my credit with Hippolyta,   75
Knowing I know thy love to Theseus?
Didst not thou lead him through the glimmering night
From Perigouna, whom he ravishèd;
And make him with fair Aegles break his faith,
With Ariadne and Antiopa?   80

forsworn – *sworn against*

Tarry – *stay*; wanton – *wilful creature*; lord – *husband*

lady – *wife*

Corin – *traditional name for a pastoral shepherd*
corn – *hay*; versing – *composing*
Phillida – *traditional name for a pastoral shepherdess*   **am**-orous (equiv. 2 syl.)
farthest step – *furthest point*   Q1 – step Q2/F – steepe (mountain)
forsooth – *in truth*; bouncing – *vigorous*
buskin'd – *in high hunting boots*   **warr**-ior (equiv. 2 syl.)

Glance at – *cast aspersions on*

                              glimm-ering (equiv. 2 syl.); Qq – not thou F – thou not
Perigouna – (see Myth)
Aegles – (see Myth)
Ariadne – (see Myth); Antiopa – (see Myth)   Source: The Life of Theseus,
                                                                        Plutarch's Lives.

TITANIA

 These are the forgeries of jealousy:
 And never, since the middle summer's spring,
 Met we on hill, in dale, forest or mead,
 By pavéd fountain, or by rushy brook,
 Or in the beachèd margent of the sea,   85
 To dance our ringlets to the whistling wind,
 But with thy brawls thou has disturb'd our sport.
 Therefore the winds, piping to us in vain,
 As in revenge have suck'd up from the sea
 Contagious fogs; which, falling in the land,   90
 Hath every pelting river made so proud
 That they have overborne their continents.
 The ox hath therefore stretch'd his yoke in vain,
 The ploughman lost his sweat, and the green corn
 Hath rotted ere his youth attain'd a beard;   95
 The fold stands empty in the drownèd field,
 And crows are fatted with the murrion flock;
 The nine-men's-morris is fill'd up with mud,
 And the quaint mazes in the wanton green
 For lack of tread are undistinguishable.   100
 The human mortals want their winter cheer:
 No night is now with hymn or carol blest.
 Therefore the moon, the governess of floods,
 Pale in her anger, washes all the air,
 That rheumatic diseases do abound.   105
 And thorough this distemperature we see
 The seasons alter: hoary-headed frosts
 Fall in the fresh lap of the crimson rose;
 And on old Hiems' thin and icy crown,

forgeries – *inventions*
the middle . . . spring – *the beginning of midsummer*
mead – *meadow*
pavéd fountain – *clear fountain with a pebbled bottom*
margent – *margin*
ringlets – *circular dances*   **whist**-ling (equiv. 2 syl.)
brawls – *fights/ dances*

As in – *In*
Contagious – *foul*
pelting – *petty*   Qq – pelting F – petty
overborne . . . continents – *overflowed*

lost his sweat – *toiled for nothing*
ere . . . beard – *before it has reached maturity*
fold – *animal pen*
murrion flock – *dead sheep*   **mur**-rion (equiv. 2 syl.)
nine-men's-morris – *diagram cut into the ground for a game played with pebbles*
quaint – *elaborate*; wanton – *overgrown*
undistinguishable – *impossible to see*   **un**-dis-**tin**-guisha–**ble** (equiv. 5 syl.)
want – *lack*   Hanmer – cheer Qq/F – heere

governess . . . floods – *(by controlling tides)*

rheumatic (metre suggests Pron. **rheu**-ma-**tic**) – *phlegmatic*
distemperature (dis-**tem**-pera-**ture**) – *loss of temper/ upset in weather*   Q1 – thorough
hoary-headed – *topped with greyish-white*   Q2/F – through

old Hiems – *Winter*   Halliwell – thin Qq/F – chin

An odorous chaplet of sweet summer buds   110
Is, as in mockery, set; the spring, the summer,
The childing autumn, angry winter, change
Their wonted liveries; and the mazèd world,
By their increase, now knows not which is which.
And this same progeny of evils comes   115
From our debate, from our dissension;
We are their parents and original.

OBERON

Do you amend it then: it lies in you.
Why should Titania cross her Oberon?
I do but beg a little changeling boy   120
To be my henchman.

TITANIA   Set your heart at rest:
The fairy land buys not the child of me.
His mother was a votress of my order;
And in the spicéd Indian air, by night,
Full often hath she gossip'd by my side;   125
And sat with me on Neptune's yellow sands,
Marking th'embarkèd traders on the flood:
When we have laugh'd to see the sails conceive
And grow big-bellied with the wanton wind;
Which she, with pretty and with swimming gait   130
Following (her womb then rich with my young squire),
Would imitate, and sail upon the land
To fetch me trifles, and return again
As from a voyage rich with merchandise.
But she, being mortal, of that boy did die;   135
And for her sake do I rear up her boy;
And for her sake I will not part with him.

chaplet – *garland*   **o**-dorous (equiv. 2 syl.)
as in mockery – *as if mocking*   **mock**-ery (equiv. 2 syl.)
childing – *fertile*
wonted – *accustomed*; mazèd – *amazed*   **liv**-eries (equiv. 2 syl.)
increase – *produce*
progency – *lineage*
debate – *quarrel*; dissension – *discord*   dis-**sen**-si-**on** (equiv. 4 syl.)
original – *origin*

amend – *mend*; lies in – *depends on*

henchman – *page of honour*

votress – *vowed female member*

Full – *very*
Neptune – (see Myth); yellow sands – *beach*
Marking – *watching*; th'embarkèd traders – *merchants*; flood – *sea*
sails . . . wind – *sails fill with wind (pregnancy metaphor)*
wanton – *playful*
swimming gait – *gliding motion*
Following – *copying*   **Follow**-ing (equiv. 2 syl.)

trifles – *small gifts*
As – *As if*
of that . . . die – *died in childbirth*   being (equiv. 1 syl.)
                                                             Qq – do I F – I do

OBERON

    How long within this wood intend you stay?

TITANIA

    Perchance till after Theseus' wedding-day.
    If you will patiently dance in our round,   140
    And see our moonlight revels, go with us;
    If not, shun me, and I will spare your haunts.

OBERON

    Give me that boy, and I will go with thee.

TITANIA

    Not for thy fairy kingdom. Fairies, away!
    We shall chide downright if I longer stay.   145

Exeunt Titania and her train.

OBERON

    Well, go thy way; thou shalt not from this grove
    Till I torment thee for this injury.
    My gentle Puck, come hither. Thou rememb'rest
    Since once I sat upon a promontory,
    And heard a mermaid on a dolphin's back   150
    Uttering such dulcet and harmonious breath
    That the rude sea grew civil at her song
    And certain stars shot madly from their spheres
    To hear the sea-maid's music?

PUCK   I remember.

OBERON

    That very time I saw (but thou couldst not),   155
    Flying between the cold moon and the earth,

intend you – *do you intend to*

Perchance – *perhaps*
patiently – *calmly*; round – *circular country dance*

shun – *avoid*; spare – *not trouble*

Fairies (equiv. 1 syl.)

chide downright – *quarrel absolutely*

from – *go from*
injury – *affront*

Since – *the time when*; promontory – *headland*

dulcet – *sweet*; breath – *song*   **Utt**-ering (equiv. 2 syl.)
rude – *rough*
spheres – *orbits*

Q1 – saw Q2/F – say

Cupid all arm'd: a certain aim he took
At a fair vestal, thronèd by the west,
And loos'd his love-shaft smartly from his bow
As it should pierce a hundred thousand hearts.   160
But I might see young Cupid's fiery shaft
Quench'd in the chaste beams of the watery moon;
And the imperial votress passed on,
In maiden meditation, fancy-free.
Yet mark'd I where the bolt of Cupid fell: 165
It fell upon a little western flower,
Before milk-white, now purple with love's wound:
And maidens call it 'love-in-idleness'.
Fetch me that flower; the herb I show'd thee once.
The juice of it, on sleeping eyelids laid,   170
Will make or man or woman madly dote
Upon the next live creature that it sees.
Fetch me this herb, and be thou here again
Ere the leviathan can swim a league.

PUCK

I'll put a girdle round about the earth   175
In forty minutes.

Exit.

OBERON   Having once this juice,
I'll watch Titania when she is asleep,
And drop the liquor of it in her eyes:
The next thing then she waking looks upon
(Be it on lion, bear, or wolf, or bull,   180
On meddling monkey, or on busy ape)
She shall pursue it with the soul of love.
And ere I take this charm from off her sight
(As I can take it with another herb)

Cupid – (see Myth); all – *fully*; certain – *accurate*

vestal – *vestal virgin (vowed to virginity)*; thronèd by – *enthroned in*

loos'd – *fired*; shaft – *arrow*; smartly – *quickly*

As it – *As if it*

might – *could*

Quench'd – *cooled down*; chaste – *celibate*   **wa**-tery (equiv. 2 syl.)

imperial votress – *vestal virgin*

fancy-free – *unmoved by love*

mark'd – *noticed*; bolt – *arrow*

purple – *blood-coloured*

'love-in-idleness' – *viola tricolour or pansy*

or ... or – *either ... or*; dote / Upon – *be in love with*

Ere – *before*; leviathan – *enormous sea monster*; league – *about 5km*

girdle – *belt*

Having once – *Once I have*

liquor – *juice*

                                                Q1 – then Q2/F – when

soul – *essence*

ere – *before*   Q1 – from off Q2/F – off from

49

I'll make her render up her page to me.   185
But who comes here? I am invisible;
And I will overhear their conference.

Enter DEMETRIUS, HELENA *following him.*

DEMETRIUS
I love thee not, therefore pursue me not.
Where is Lysander and fair Hermia?
The one I'll slay, the other slayeth me.   190
Thou told'st me they were stol'n unto this wood;
And here am I, and wood within this wood
Because I cannot meet my Hermia.
Hence, get thee gone, and follow me no more.

HELENA
You draw me, you hard-hearted adamant –   195
But yet you draw not iron, for my heart
Is true as steel. Leave you your power to draw,
And I shall have no power to follow you.

DEMETRIUS
Do I entice you? Do I speak you fair?
Or rather do I not in plainest truth   200
Tell you I do not, nor I cannot love you?

HELENA
And even for that do I love you the more.
I am your spaniel; and, Demetrius,
The more you beat me, I will fawn on you.
Use me but as your spaniel, spurn me, strike me,   205
Neglect me, lose me; only give me leave,
Unworthy as I am, to follow you.
What worser place can I beg in your love –

render up – *give up*

con-fer-**ence** (equiv. 3 syl.)

is – *are*
The ... slay – *I'll kill Lysander*; the other ... me – *Hermia kills me*
stol'n (equiv. 1 syl.); Q1 – unto Q2/F – into
and wood – *and mad with anger*

draw me – *attract*; adamant – *magnet*
but yet ... iron – *you don't draw iron (particularly susceptible to magnets)*
Leave you – *Give up*; draw – *attract*   heart ... steel – Prov.

entice – *allure*; speak you fair – *speak kindly to you*

even (equiv. 1 syl.); Q1 – you Q2/F – thee
I ... on you – Prov.
fawn on – *behave affectionately to*
but – *only*
leave – *permission*

And yet a place of high respect with me –
Than to be usèd as you use your dog?   210

DEMETRIUS

Tempt not too much the hatred of my spirit;
For I am sick when I do look on thee.

HELENA

And I am sick when I look not on you.

DEMETRIUS

You do impeach your modesty too much
To leave the city and commit yourself   215
Into the hands of one that loves you not,
To trust the opportunity of night
And the ill counsel of a desert place
With the rich worth of your virginity.

HELENA

Your virtue is my privilege: for that   220
It is not night when I do see your face,
Therefore I think I am not in the night;
Nor doth this wood lack worlds of company,
For you, in my respect, are all the world;
Then how can it be said I am alone,   225
When all the world is here to look on me?

DEMETRIUS

I'll run from thee and hide me in the brakes,
And leave thee to the mercy of wild beasts.

HELENA

The wildest hath not such a heart as you.

usèd – *treated*   Qq – use F – do

the hatred of my spirit – *my feelings of hatred*
do look – *look*

impeach – *discredit*
To leave – *by leaving*

opportunity – *circumstances*
ill counsel – *bad intentions*; desert – *isolated*

privilege – *safeguard*; for that – *because*

Punct. Rowe – face, Qq f – face.

doth – *does*; worlds of company – *the company of all the world*
in my respect – *to my mind*

brakes – *bushes*

Run when you will; the story shall be chang'd: 230
Apollo flies, and Daphne holds the chase;
The dove pursues the griffin, the mild hind
Makes speed to catch the tiger – bootless speed,
When cowardice pursues and valour flies!

DEMETRIUS

I will not stay thy questions; let me go,   235
Or if thou follow me, do not believe
But I shall do thee mischief in the wood.

HELENA

Ay, in the temple, in the town, the field,
You do me mischief. Fie, Demetrius!
Your wrongs do set a scandal on my sex.   240
We cannot fight for love, as men may do;
We should be woo'd, and were not made to woo.

[Exit Demetrius.]

I'll follow thee, and make a heaven of hell,
To die upon the hand I love so well.

Exit.

OBERON

Fare thee well, nymph; ere he do leave this grove   245
Thou shalt fly him, and he shall seek thy love.

Enter PUCK.

Hast thou the flower there? Welcome, wanderer.

will – *want*

Apollo ... chase – *(reverses the myth)* (see Myth)   Source: Ovid, *Metamorphosis*

griffin – *mythical creature, half lion, half eagle*; hind – *female deer*

bootless – *useless*

valour – *bravery*

stay – *wait for*

do not ... But – *believe that*

mischief – *harm*

Q1 – the field Q2/F – and field

do ... sex – *make me behave in a manner that disgraces my sex*

heaven (equiv. 1 syl.); Qq – I'll F – I

upon – *by*

ere – *before*

fly – *flee from*

flower (equiv. 1 syl.)

PUCK
   Ay, there it is.

OBERON   I pray thee give it me.
   I know a bank where the wild thyme blows,
   Where oxlips and the nodding violet grows,   250
   Quite over-canopied with luscious woodbine,
   With sweet musk-roses, and with eglantine.
   There sleeps Titania sometime of the night,
   Lull'd in these flowers with dances and delight;
   And there the snake throws her enamell'd skin,   255
   Weed wide enough to wrap a fairy in;
   And with the juice of this I'll streak her eyes,
   And make her full of hateful fantasies.
   Take thou some of it, and seek through this grove:
   A sweet Athenian lady is in love   260
   With a disdainful youth; anoint his eyes;
   But do it when the next thing he espies
   May be the lady. Thou shalt know the man
   By the Athenian garments he hath on.
   Effect it with some care, that he may prove   265
   More fond on her than she upon her love:
   And look thou meet me ere the first cock crow.

PUCK
   Fear not, my lord, your servant shall do so.

                    Exeunt

Rhyme – lines 249–268 are in rhyming couplets

Metre – line is short by 1 syl. (whe-**re** might be pronounced as 2 syl.).

oxlips – *flowers, a cross between a primrose and a cowslip.*

Quite – *completely*; woodbine – *honeysuckle*

musk-roses – *climbing roses*; eglantine – *sweet briar*

sometime – *for some part*

Lull'd – *put to sleep*   flowers (equiv. 1 syl.)

throws – *casts off*

Weed – *garment*

streak – *smear*

espies – *sees*

Effect it – *Do it*

fond on – *in love with*

ere – *before*

ACT 2, SCENE 2

Enter TITANIA, *Queen of Fairies, with her train.*

TITANIA

 Come, now a roundel and a fairy song;
 Then for the third part of a minute, hence:
 Some to kill cankers in the musk-rose buds;
 Some war with reremice for their leathern wings,
 To make my small elves coats; and some keep back   5
 The clamorous owl, that nightly hoots and wonders
 At our quaint spirits. Sing me now asleep;
 Then to your offices, and let me rest.

The Fairies sing.

1 FAIRY

 You spotted snakes with double tongue,
 Thorny hedgehogs, be not seen;   10
 Newts and blind-worms, do no wrong,
 Come not near our fairy queen.

CHORUS

 Philomel, with melody,
 Sing in our sweet lullaby;
 Lulla, lulla, lullaby; lulla, lulla, lullaby;   15
 Never harm, nor spell, nor charm,
 Come our lovely lady nigh;
 So goodnight, with lullaby.

1 FAIRY

 Weaving spiders, come not here;
 Hence, you long-legg'd spinners, hence!   20

roundel – *circular dance*
for . . . minute – *in twenty seconds*
cankers – *worms*
reremice – *bats*; leathern – *leathery*   **rere**-mice (equiv. two syl.) – Pron. – **reer**-mice

clamorous – *noisy*   **clam**-orous (equiv. 2 syl.)
quaint – *strange*
offices – *duties*

double – *forked*

blind-worms – *adders*

Philomel – *nightingale* (see Myth)   Source: Ovid, *Metamorphosis*
                                            Qq – our F – your

Come . . . nigh – *come near our lady*

                              Qq – 1 FAIRY F – 2 FAIRY

Beetles black, approach not near;
Worm nor snail, do no offence.

CHORUS
Philomel, with melody, etc.

[Titania sleeps.]

2 FAIRY
Hence, away! Now all is well;
One aloof stand sentinel.   25

[Exeunt Fairies.]

Enter OBERON, [and squeezes the juice on Titania's eyelids.]

OBERON
What thou seest when thou dost wake,
Do it for thy true love take;
Love and languish for his sake.
Be it ounce, or cat, or bear,
Pard, or boar with bristled hair,   30
In thy eye that shall appear
When thou wak'st, it is thy dear.
Wake when some vile thing is near.

[Exit.]

Enter LYSANDER and HERMIA.

LYSANDER
Fair love, you faint with wand'ring in the wood,
And, to speak troth, I have forgot our way.   35

offence – *harm*

Philomel, with melody, etc. – Chorus is repeated

Qq – 2 FAIRY F – 1 FAIRY

aloof – *at a distance*; sentinel – *guard*

Metre – the lines are in catalectic trochaic tetrameter – see Introduction –
Do . . . take – *Take it to be your true love*   Magic Metre

ounce – *lynx*
Pard – *leopard*
In . . . appear – *That appears before you*

Q1 – wood Q2/F – woods; Rhyme – Lysander begins in alternate rhyming lines
troth – *truth*

We'll rest us, Hermia, if you think it good,
And tarry for the comfort of the day.

HERMIA

Be it so, Lysander: find you out a bed,
For I upon this bank will rest my head.

LYSANDER

One turf shall serve as pillow for us both;   40
One heart, one bed, two bosoms, and one troth.

HERMIA

Nay, good Lysander; for my sake, my dear,
Lie further off yet; do not lie so near.

LYSANDER

O take the sense, sweet, of my innocence!
Love takes the meaning in love's conference.   45
I mean that my heart unto yours is knit,
So that but one heart we can make of it:
Two bosoms interchainèd with an oath,
So then, two bosoms and a single troth.
Then by your side no bed-room me deny;   50
For lying so, Hermia, I do not lie.

HERMIA

Lysander riddles very prettily.
Now much beshrew my manners and my pride,
If Hermia meant to say Lysander lied!
But, gentle friend, for love and courtesy,   55
Lie further off, in human modesty;
Such separation as may well be said
Becomes a virtuous bachelor and a maid,

tarry – *wait*

Rhyme – the dialogue moves into rhyming couplets

Be it so – *So be it*   Be it **so** (anapest – see 'a Note on Metre')

troth – *pledge*

take the sense – *take the true meaning*
Love . . . conference – *Lovers understand*   **con**-fer-**ence** (equiv. 3 syl.)
one another when they speak
So that but – *So that*   Qq – we can F – can you
interchainèd – *linked with one another*   Qq – interchained F – interchanged
troth – *pledge*
no . . . deny – *Don't deny me a sleeping place*
lying – *lying down*; lie – *deceive*   lying (equiv. 1 syl.)

prettily – *cleverly*
beshrew – *curse*
lied – *deceived*
friend – *lover*
human – *polite*

vir-tuous (equiv. 2 syl.); **bach**-elor (equiv. 2 syl.)

So far be distant; and good night, sweet friend:
Thy love ne'er alter till thy sweet life end!   60

LYSANDER
Amen, amen, to that fair prayer say I;
And then end life when I end loyalty!
Here is my bed; sleep give thee all his rest.

HERMIA
With half that wish the wisher's eyes be press'd.

They sleep.

Enter PUCK.

PUCK
Through the forest have I gone;   65
But Athenian found I none
On whose eyes I might approve
This flower's force in stirring love.
Night and silence – Who is here?
Weeds of Athens he doth wear: 70
This is he my master said
Despiséd the Athenian maid;
And here the maiden, sleeping sound,
On the dank and dirty ground.
Pretty soul, she durst not lie   75
Near this lack-love, this kill-courtesy.
Churl, upon thy eyes I throw
All the power this charm doth owe:
When thou wak'st, let love forbid
Sleep his seat on thy eyelid.   80
So awake when I am gone;

prayer (equiv. 1 syl.)

the ... press'd – *may your eyes be closed in sleep*

Metre – Puck's speech is in rhyming tetrameter couplets – see Intro. – Magic Metre.

Q1 – found Q2/F – find

approve – *test*

Night and silence – *(an exclamation)*
Weeds – *clothes*

durst – *dares*

Metre – this line is nine syllables in length

Churl – *miser*
owe – *possess*
forbid ... eyelid – *banish sleep from your eyes*

For I must now to Oberon.

Exit.

Enter DEMETRIUS and HELENA, running.

HELENA
Stay, though thou kill me, sweet Demetrius!

DEMETRIUS
I charge thee, hence, and do not haunt me thus.

HELENA
O wilt thou darkling leave me? Do not so.   85

DEMETRIUS
Stay, on thy peril; I alone will go.

Exit.

HELENA
O, I am out of breath in this fond chase!
The more my prayer, the lesser is my grace.
Happy is Hermia, wheresoe'er she lies,
For she hath blessèd and attractive eyes.   90
How came her eyes so bright? Not with salt tears;
If so, my eyes are oftener wash'd than hers.
No, no; I am as ugly as a bear,
For beasts that meet me run away for fear:
Therefore no marvel though Demetrius   95
Do, as a monster, fly my presence thus.
What wicked and dissembling glass of mine
Made me compare with Hermia's sphery eyne?
But who is here? Lysander, on the ground?

to – *go to*

Rhyme – Helena and Demetrius join the other lovers in speaking in rhyming couplets.

charge – *command*; haunt me – *hang about me*

darkling – *in the dark*

on thy – *at thy*

fond – *foolish*
the ... grace – *the less favour I win*
wheresoe'er – *wherever*; lies – *is*

oft-ener (equiv. 2 syl.)

no marvel though – *no wonder that*
Do – *Does*; as – *as if from*
dissembling – *deceiving*; glass – *mirror*
compare – *compare myself*; sphery eyne – *star-like eyes*

Dead, or asleep? I see no blood, no wound.   100
Lysander, if you live, good sir, awake!

LYSANDER [*waking*]
And run through fire I will for thy sweet sake!
Transparent Helena! Nature shows art,
That through thy bosom makes me see thy heart.
Where is Demetrius? O how fit a word   105
Is that vile name to perish on my sword!

HELENA
Do not say so, Lysander, say not so.
What though he love your Hermia? Lord, what
    though?
Yet Hermia still loves you; then be content.

LYSANDER
Content with Hermia? No. I do repent   110
The tedious minutes I with her have spent.
Not Hermia, but Helena I love:
Who will not change a raven for a dove?
The will of man is by his reason sway'd,
And reason says you are the worthier maid.   115
Things growing are not ripe until their season:
So I, being young, till now ripe not to reason;
And, touching now the point of human skill,
Reason becomes the marshal to my will,
And leads me to your eyes, where I o'erlook   120
Love's stories, written in love's richest book.

HELENA
Wherefore was I to this keen mockery born?
When at your hands did I deserve this scorn?
Is't not enough, is't not enough, young man,

Transparent – *see-through/radiant (double meaning)*; shows art – *has magic powers*

fit – *suitable*

What though – *what of it if*

ted-ious (equiv. 2 syl.)

Q1 – I love Qq/F – now I

will – *desire (with sexual pun)*

wor-thier (equiv. 2 syl.)

ripe . . . reason – *haven't matured to see reason*
touching . . . point – *reaching the peak*; skill – *reason*
marshal to – *officer of*
o'erlook – *read*

Wherefore – *Why*; keen – *bitter*

mock-ery (equiv. 2 syl.)

That I did never, no, nor never can 125
Deserve a sweet look from Demetrius' eye,
But you must flout my insufficiency?
Good troth, you do me wrong, good sooth, you do,
In such disdainful manner me to woo.
But fare you well; perforce I must confess 130
I thought you lord of more true gentleness.
O that a lady, of one man refus'd,
Should of another therefore be abus'd!

Exit.

LYSANDER
 She sees not Hermia. Hermia, sleep thou there,
 And never mayst thou come Lysander near! 135
 For, as a surfeit of the sweetest things
 The deepest loathing to the stomach brings;
 Or as the heresies that men do leave
 Are hated most of those they did deceive;
 So thou, my surfeit and my heresy, 140
 Of all be hated, but the most of me!
 And, all my powers, address your love and might
 To honour Helen, and to be her knight!

Exit.

HERMIA [*starting*]
 Help me, Lysander, help me! Do thy best
 To pluck this crawling serpent from my breast! 145
 Ay me, for pity! What a dream was here!
 Lysander, look how I do quake with fear.
 Methought a serpent ate my heart away,
 And you sat smiling at his cruel prey.

flout – *mock*; insufficiency – *incompetence*
troth – *truth*; good sooth – *indeed*
me to woo – *to woo me*
perforce – *necessarily*
gentleness – *nobility*
of – *by*
of – *by*

sees not – *doesn't see*
never mayst thou – *may you never*
a surfeit – *an excess*
For . . . brings – *As too many sweet things make one sick*
heresies – *false teachings*; leave – *reject*
of – *by*   Qq – they F – that

Of – *by*
address – *direct*   powers (equiv. 1 syl.)

Methought – *I thought*
prey – *preying*   **cru**-el (equiv. 2 syl.)

Lysander! What, remov'd? Lysander! lord!   150
What, out of hearing? Gone? No sound, no word?
Alack, where are you? Speak, and if you hear;
Speak, of all loves. I swoon almost with fear.
No? Then I well perceive you are not nigh.
Either death or you I'll find immediately.   155

Exit.

ACT 3, SCENE 1

[Titania still lying asleep.]
Enter QUINCE, BOTTOM, SNUG, FLUTE, SNOUT *and* STARVELING.

BOTTOM
Are we all met?

QUINCE
Pat, pat; and here's a marvellous convenient
place for our rehearsal. This green plot shall be our
stage, this hawthorn-brake our tiring-house; and we
will do it in action, as we will do it before the Duke.   5

BOTTOM
Peter Quince!

QUINCE
What sayest thou, bully Bottom?

BOTTOM
There are things in this comedy of Pyramus
and Thisbe that will never please. First, Pyramus must
draw a sword to kill himself; which the ladies cannot   10
abide. How answer you that?

remov'd – *departed*

of all loves – *for love's sake*
nigh – *near*

Pat, pat – *on the dot*; convenient – *suitable*

hawthorn-brake – *hawthorn bush*

bully – *gallant (term of endearment)*

SNOUT

Byrlakin, a parlous fear.

STARVELING

I believe we must leave the killing out,
when all is done.

BOTTOM

Not a whit; I have a device to make all well.   15
Write me a prologue, and let the prologue seem to say
we will do no harm with our swords, and that Pyramus
is not killed indeed; and for the more better assurance,
tell them that I, Pyramus, am not Pyramus, but
Bottom the weaver. This will put them out of   20
fear.

QUINCE

Well, we will have such a prologue; and it shall
be written in eight and six.

BOTTOM

No, make it two more; let it be written in eight and
eight.   25

SNOUT

Will not the ladies be afeard of the lion?

STARVELING

I fear it, I promise you.

BOTTOM

Masters, you ought to consider with yourself;
to bring in (God shield us!) a lion among ladies is a
most dreadful thing; for there is not a more fearful   30

Byrlakin – *By our ladykin (the Virgin Mary)*; parlous – *perilous*

whit – *bit*

for the more better assurance – *to reassure them more fully*

put them out of fear – *free them from fear*

eight and six – *alternate lines of eight and six syllables*

afeard – *afraid*

it – *the lion/the ladies' fear*

Qq – yourself F – yourselves

fearful – *fearsome*

wild-fowl than your lion living; and we ought to look
to't.

SNOUT

Therefore another prologue must tell he is not a
lion.

BOTTOM

Nay, you must name his name, and half his   35
face must be seen through the lion's neck; and he
himself must speak through, saying thus, or to the
same defect: 'Ladies,' or 'Fair ladies, I would wish
you,' or 'I would request you,' or 'I would entreat you,
not to fear, not to tremble: my life for yours! If you   40
think I come hither as a lion, it were pity of my life.
No, I am no such thing; I am a man, as other men
are': and there, indeed, let him name his name, and
tell them plainly he is Snug the joiner.

QUINCE

Well, it shall be so. But there is two hard things: 45
that is, to bring the moonlight into a chamber; for
you know, Pyramus and Thisbe meet by moonlight.

SNOUT

Doth the moon shine that night we play our play?

BOTTOM

A calendar, a calendar! Look in the almanac;
find out moonshine, find out moonshine!   50

QUINCE

Yes, it doth shine that night.

look to't – *look at it*

Q1 – to't Q2/F – to it

defect – *(malapropism for 'effect')*

my life for yours – *by my life*
hither – *here*; pity of my life – *my life would be in danger*

almanac – *calendar of tides/moons, etc.*
find out moonshine –   This is the point given in F for Puck's entrance.
find out when the moon shines

BOTTOM

Why, then may you leave a casement of the
great chamber window, where we play, open; and the
moon may shine in at the casement.

QUINCE

Ay; or else one must come in with a bush of   55
thorns and a lantern, and say he comes to disfigure or
to present the person of Moonshine. Then there is
another thing: we must have a wall in the great
chamber; for Pyramus and Thisbe, says the story, did
talk through the chink of a wall.   60

SNOUT

You can never bring in a wall. What say you,
Bottom?

BOTTOM

Some man or other must present Wall; and let
him have some plaster, or some loam, or some
roughcast about him, to signify wall; and let him hold   65
his fingers thus, and through that cranny shall
Pyramus and Thisbe whisper.

QUINCE

If that may be, then all is well. Come sit down,
every mother's son, and rehearse your parts. Pyramus,
you begin: when you have spoken your speech,   70
enter into that brake; and so every one according to
his cue.

casement – *section of a window*

bush . . . lantern – *traditional properties of the man in the moon*
disfigure – *malapropism for 'figure'*
present – *personate*

chink – *narrow opening*

loam – *soil of clay and sand*
roughcast – *coarse plaster containing lime*
cranny – *opening*

every mother's son – *everyone* (Prov.)

brake – *thicket*

Enter PUCK.

PUCK
What hempen homespuns have we swaggering here,
So near the cradle of the Fairy Queen?
What, a play toward? I'll be an auditor;   75
An actor too perhaps, if I see cause.

QUINCE
Speak, Pyramus; Thisbe, stand forth.

BOTTOM
Thisbe, the flowers of odious savours sweet —

QUINCE
'Odorous'! 'odorous'!

BOTTOM
Odorous savours sweet;   80
So hath thy breath, my dearest Thisbe dear.
But hark, a voice! Stay thou but here awhile,
And by and by I will to thee appear.

Exit.

PUCK
A stranger Pyramus than e'er played here!

[Exit.]

FLUTE
Must I speak now?   85

hempen homespuns – *rustics wearing hemp*

cradle – *resting place*

toward – *impending*; auditor – *listener*

swagg-ering (equiv.2 syl.)

What, a **play** (anapest)

flowers (equiv. 1 syl.); **o**-dious (equiv. 2 syl.)

odorous – *sweet smelling*

Cunningham – 'Odorous'! 'odorous'! Qq – Odours, odorous F – Odours, odours

Brooks – Odorous Qq/F – Odours; **O**-dorous (equiv. 2 syl.)

by and by – *in a moment*

SP – F – PUCK Qq – QUINCE

QUINCE

Ay, marry, must you; for you must understand
he goes but to see a noise that he heard, and is to come
again.

FLUTE

Most radiant Pyramus, most lily-white of hue,
Of colour like the red rose on triumphant briar,   90
Most brisky juvenal, and eke most lovely Jew,
As true as truest horse that yet would never tire;
I'll meet thee, Pyramus, at Ninny's tomb.

QUINCE

'Ninus' tomb', man! Why, you must not speak
that yet; that you answer to Pyramus. You speak all   95
your part at once, cues and all.
Pyramus, enter! Your cue is past; it is 'never tire'.

FLUTE

O – As true as truest horse that yet would never tire.

Enter [PUCK, and] BOTTOM with the ass-head [on].

BOTTOM

If I were fair, Thisbe, I were only thine.

QUINCE

O monstrous! O strange! We are haunted! Pray,   100
masters! Fly, masters! Help!

Exeunt Quince, Snug, Flute, Snout and Starveling.

marry – *indeed*
see a noise – *(confusion of the senses)*

hue – *colour*   Metre – iambic hexameter – see Intro. – Metre of
triumphant – *glorious*   Pyramus and Thisbe
brisky – *lively*; juvenal – *youth*; eke – *also*; Jew – *term of affection*
As . . . tire – *Like the most unweariable and willing horse*

Ninus – (see Myth)

part – *(Elizabethan actors had only a part containing their lines and a few cue words)*

were – *would be*   Bottom punctuates this line wrongly – the meaning is surely
                          'If I were, fair Thisbe, I were only thine'.

PUCK

I'll follow you: I'll lead you about a round!
Through bog, through bush, through brake, through
    briar;
Sometime a horse I'll be, sometime a hound,
A hog, a headless bear, sometime a fire;   105
And neigh, and bark, and grunt, and roar, and burn,
Like horse, hound, hog, bear, fire, at every turn.

Exit.

BOTTOM

Why do they run away? This is a knavery of
them to make me afeard.

Enter SNOUT.

SNOUT

O Bottom, thou art changed! What do I see on   110
thee?

BOTTOM

What do you see? You see an ass-head of your
own, do you?   *[Exit Snout.]*

Enter QUINCE.

QUINCE

Bless thee, Bottom, bless thee! Thou art translated.   115

Exit.

Rhyme – alternate rhyming lines followed by a couplet;

a round – *a circular dance/ in a circle*   you a-**bout** (anapest – see 'A Note on Metre')

Metre – this line is short by 2 syl.

knavery – *trick*

translated – *transformed*

BOTTOM

I see their knavery: this is to make an ass of
me, to fright me, if they could. But I will not stir from
this place, do what they can; I will walk up and down
here, and I will sing, that they shall hear I am not
afraid.   120

[*Sings.*] *The ousel cock, so black of hue,*
With orange-tawny bill,
The throstle, with his note so true,
The wren with little quill –

[*The singing awakens Titania.*]

TITANIA

What angel wakes me from my flowery bed?   125

BOTTOM [*Sings.*]

The finch, the sparrow, and the lark,
The plain-song cuckoo gray,
Whose note full many a man doth mark,
And dares not answer nay –

for indeed, who would set his wit to so foolish a bird?   130
Who would give a bird the lie, though he cry 'cuckoo'
never so?

TITANIA

I pray thee, gentle mortal, sing again:
Mine ear is much enamour'd of thy note;
So is mine eye enthrallèd to thy shape;   135
And thy fair virtue's force perforce doth move me
On the first view to say, to swear, I love thee.

BOTTOM

Methinks, mistress, you should have little

knavery – *trickery*

ousel cock – *male blackbird*

throstle – *song thrush*
quill – *pipe/shrill sound*   Qq – with F – and

Metre – Titania speaks in VERSE whilst Bottom speaks in PROSE

plain-song – *with simple song*
mark – *notice*
dares . . . nay – *does not dare to answer the accusation of 'cuckoo' (cuckold)*
      'who . . . bird?' – Prov. – variation on 'do not set your wit against a fool'
give . . . lie – *accuse the bird of lying*; cuckoo – *cuckold (man with an unfaithful wife)*
never so – *ever so much*

perforce – *forcibly*

reason for that. And yet, to say the truth, reason and
love keep little company together nowadays. The more   140
the pity that some honest neighbours will not make
them friends. Nay, I can gleek upon occasion.

TITANIA
Thou art as wise as thou art beautiful.

BOTTOM
Not so neither; but if I had wit enough to get
out of this wood, I have enough to serve mine own turn.   145

TITANIA
Out of this wood do not desire to go:
Thou shalt remain here, whether thou wilt or no.
I am a spirit of no common rate;
The summer still doth tend upon my state;
And I do love thee: therefore go with me.   150
I'll give thee fairies to attend on thee;
And they shall fetch thee jewels from the deep,
And sing, while thou on pressèd flowers dost sleep:
And I will purge thy mortal grossness so,
That thou shalt like an airy spirit go.   155
Peaseblossom! Cobweb! Moth! and Mustardseed!

Enter four fairies: PEASEBLOSSOM, COBWEB, MOTH and
MUSTARDSEED.

PEASEBLOSSOM
Ready.

COBWEB   And I.

MOTH   And I.

gleek – *jest*; upon occasion – *as the occasion arises*

turn – *purposes*

Rhyme – rhyming couplets

wilt or no – *want to or not*   whether (equiv. 1 syl)

rate – *value*

still – *always*; tend upon – *serve*; state – *status as queen*

deep – *bottom of the sea*

purge – *rid you of*; mortal grossness – *human form*

Metre – irregular shared line (12 syl.)

MUSTARDSEED   And I.

ALL   Where shall we go?

TITANIA
Be kind and courteous to this gentleman;
Hop in his walks, and gambol in his eyes;
Feed him with apricocks and dewberries,   160
With purple grapes, green figs, and mulberries;
The honey-bags steal from the humble-bees,
And for night-tapers crop their waxen thighs,
And light them at the fiery glow-worms' eyes,
To have my love to bed, and to arise;   165
And pluck the wings from painted butterflies
To fan the moonbeams from his sleeping eyes.
Nod to him, elves, and do him courtesies.

PEASEBLOSSOM
Hail, mortal!

COBWEB
Hail!   170

MOTH
Hail!

MUSTARDSEED
Hail!

BOTTOM
I cry your worships mercy, heartily. I beseech
your worship's name?

cour-teous (equiv. 2 syl.)
gambol – play; eyes – sight   Rhyme – the rest of the speech is in rhyming couplets
apricocks – apricots; dewberries – blackberries

humble-bees – bumble bees
night-tapers – candles; crop – cut off; waxen thighs – legs of wax

have – lead; arise – get up/ get an erection

Nod – give sign of assent

cry . . . mercy – beg your pardon

COBWEB

    Cobweb.   175

BOTTOM

    I shall desire you of more acquaintance, good
    Master Cobweb: if I cut my finger, I shall make bold
    with you. Your name, honest gentleman?

PEASEBLOSSOM

    Peaseblossom.

BOTTOM

    I pray you, commend me to Mistress Squash, your   180
    mother, and to Master Peascod, your father. Good
    Master Peaseblossom, I shall desire you of more
    acquaintance too. Your name, I beseech you sir?

MUSTARDSEED

    Mustardseed.

BOTTOM

    Good Master Mustardseed, I know your   185
    patience well. That same cowardly giant-like ox-beef
    hath devoured many a gentleman of your house: I
    promise you, your kindred hath made my eyes water
    ere now. I desire you of more acquaintance, good
    Master Mustardseed.   190

TITANIA

    Come, wait upon him; lead him to my bower.
    The moon, methinks, looks with a watery eye,
    And when she weeps, weeps every little flower,
    Lamenting some enforcèd chastity.

desire ... acquaintance – *wish to become better acquainted with you*
if I cut my finger – *(cobweb could be used as a form of plaster)*

Squash – *unripe pea pod*
Peascod – *pea pod*

Qq – you of F – of you

patience – *endurance*; giant ... house – *(mustard is eaten with beef)*

made ... water – *(with the heat of mustard)*

bower (equiv. 1 syl.)
wat-ery (equiv 2 syl.)

weeps – *causing dew (thought to originate with the moon)*
enforcèd – *violated by force*

Tie up my love's tongue, bring him silently.   195

Exeunt.

ACT 3, SCENE 2

Enter OBERON, *King of Fairies.*

OBERON
I wonder if Titania be awak'd;
Then, what it was that next came in her eye,
Which she must dote on in extremity.

Enter PUCK.

Here comes my messenger. How now, mad spirit?
What night-rule now about this haunted grove?   5

PUCK
My mistress with a monster is in love.
Near to her close and consecrated bower,
While she was in her dull and sleeping hour,
A crew of patches, rude mechanicals,
That work for bread upon Athenian stalls,   10
Were met together to rehearse a play
Intended for great Theseus' nuptial day.
The shallowest thick-skin of that barren sort,
Who Pyramus presented in their sport,
Forsook his scene, and enter'd in a brake,   15
When I did him at this advantage take:
An ass's nole I fixèd on his head.
Anon, his Thisbe must be answeréd,
And forth my mimic comes. When they him spy –

Pope – love's Qq/F – lovers

in extremity – *to an extreme level*

night-rule – *activities of the night*; haunted – *much frequented*

Punct. Rowe – in love. Qq/F – in love,
close – *secluded*; consecrated – *sacred*   Punct. Rowe/Q2/F – bower, Q1 – bower.
dull – *inactive*   Rhyme – the scene moves into rhyming couplets
patches – *clowns*; rude – *uneducated/ coarse*; mechanicals – *manual workers*

shallowest (**shallow**-est) – *stupidest*; thick-skin – *one lacking feeling*; barren sort –
sport – *entertainment*   *witless group*
Forsook – *exited*; enter'd in a brake – *went into a thicket*

nole – *head*
Anon – *Shortly*
mimic – *actor*; spy – *see*

As wild geese that the creeping fowler eye,   20
Or russet-pated choughs, many in sort,
Rising and cawing at the gun's report,
Sever themselves, and madly sweep the sky
So, at his sight, away his fellows fly;
And at our stamp, here o'er and o'er one falls;   25
He murder cries, and help from Athens calls.
Their sense thus weak, lost with their fears thus strong,
Made senseless things begin to do them wrong:
For briars and thorns at their apparel snatch;
Some sleeves, some hats, from yielders all things catch.   30
I led them on in this distracted fear,
And left sweet Pyramus translated there;
When in that moment, so it came to pass,
Titania wak'd, and straightway lov'd an ass.

OBERON
   This falls out better than I could devise.   35
   But hast thou yet latch'd the Athenian's eyes
   With the love-juice, as I did bid thee do?

PUCK
   I took him sleeping – that is finish'd too –
   And the Athenian woman by his side,
   That when he wak'd, of force she must be ey'd.   40

       Enter DEMETRIUS and HERMIA.

OBERON
   Stand close: this is the same Athenian.

PUCK
   This is the woman, but not this the man.
   [*They stand apart.*]

fowler – *hunter*; eye – *see*
russet-pated – *reddish-brown headed*; choughs – *jackdaws*   choughs – Pron. – chuffs
report – *sound of firing*
Sever – *scatter*; sweep – *sweep across*

at our stamp – *when I stamped*
He – *One*

senseless – *inanimate*
apparel – *clothing*
from yielders all things catch – *everything robs those who yield to fear*

translated – *transformed*

falls out – *has worked out*
latch'd – *moistened*

That – *so that*; of force – *by necessity*; ey'd – *seen*

close – *concealed*

DEMETRIUS

    O why rebuke you him that loves you so?
    Lay breath so bitter on your bitter foe.

HERMIA

    Now I but chide, but I should use thee worse,   45
    For thou, I fear, hast given me cause to curse.
    If thou hast slain Lysander in his sleep,
    Being o'er shoes in blood, plunge in the deep,
    And kill me too.
    The sun was not so true unto the day   50
    As he to me. Would he have stol'n away
    From sleeping Hermia? I'll believe as soon
    This whole earth may be bor'd, and that the moon
    May through the centre creep, and so displease
    Her brother's noon-tide with th'Antipodes.   55
    It cannot be but thou hast murder'd him:
    So should a murderer look, so dead, so grim.

DEMETRIUS

    So should the murder'd look, and so should I,
    Pierc'd through the heart with your stern cruelty;
    Yet you, the murderer, look as bright, as clear,   60
    As yonder Venus in her glimmering sphere.

HERMIA

    What's this to my Lysander? Where is he?
    Ah, good Demetrius, wilt thou give him me?

DEMETRIUS

    I had rather give his carcase to my hounds.

but chide – *only scold;* use – *treat*

given (equiv. 1 syl.)

o'er shoes in blood – *knee deep in blood* (Prov.)

Metre – this line is short by 6 syl.

whole – *solid;* bor'd – *bored through*
displease – *by bringing night with it*
Her brother's – *The sun's;* Antipodes – *those living on the opposite side of the earth*
but – *other than that*
dead – *deadly pale*

mur-derer (equiv. 2 syl.)

Qq – murder'd F – murderer

mur-derer (equiv. 2 syl.)

sphere – *hollow globe thought to surround planets*

glimm-ering (equiv. 2 syl.)

to – *to do with*

I had (equiv. 1 syl); Q1 – I had Q2/F – I'd

HERMIA

    Out, dog! Out, cur! Thou driv'st me past the bounds   65
    Of maiden's patience. Hast thou slain him then?
    Henceforth be never number'd among men!
    O once tell true; tell true, even for my sake!
    Durst thou have look'd upon him, being awake,
    And hast thou kill'd him sleeping? O brave touch!   70
    Could not a worm, an adder, do so much?
    An adder did it; for with doubler tongue
    Than thine, thou serpent, never adder stung!

DEMETRIUS

    You spend your passion on a mispris'd mood:
    I am not guilty of Lysander's blood;   75
    Nor is he dead, for aught that I can tell.

HERMIA

    I pray thee tell me then that he is well.

DEMETRIUS

    And if I could, what should I get therefor?

HERMIA

    A privilege, never to see me more.
    And from thy hated presence part I so: 80
    See me no more, whether he be dead or no.   *Exit.*

DEMETRIUS

    There is no following her in this fierce vein;
    Here therefore for a while I will remain.
    So sorrow's heaviness doth heavier grow
    For debt that bankrupt sleep doth sorrow owe;   85
    Which now in some slight measure it will pay,
    If for his tender here I make some stay.

bounds – *boundaries*

number'd – *counted*
once tell true – *tell the truth once and for all*
Durst thou – *Would you dare*   being (equiv. 1 syl.)
brave touch – *fine action*
worm – *serpent*
doubler – *more forked/ deceitful*   **doub**-ler (equiv. 2 syl.)
never . . . stung – *no adder ever stung*

spend – *expend*; mispris'd – *mistaken*; mood – *anger*
guilty of – *guilty of spilling*
aught – *anything*

therefor – *for that*

no – *not*   whether (equiv. 1 syl.)

vein – *mood*   **foll**-owing (equiv. 2 syl.)

So . . . owe – *So sorrow grows heavier as a result of lack of sleep*

tender – *sleep's offer*; make some stay – *stay here a while*

Lies down [and sleeps]. Oberon and Puck come forward.

OBERON

 What hast thou done? Thou hast mistaken quite,
 And laid the love-juice on some true love's sight;
 Of thy misprision must perforce ensue   90
 Some true love turn'd, and not a false turn'd true.

PUCK

 Then fate o'er-rules, that, one man holding troth,
 A million fail, confounding oath on oath.

OBERON

 About the wood go swifter than the wind,
 And Helena of Athens look thou find;   95
 All fancy-sick she is, and pale of cheer
 With sighs of love, that costs the fresh blood dear.
 By some illusion see thou bring her here;
 I'll charm his eyes against she do appear.

PUCK

 I go, I go, look how I go!   100
 Swifter than arrow from the Tartar's bow.   *Exit.*

OBERON

 [*Squeezing the juice on Demetrius' eyelids.*]
 Flower of this purple dye,
 Hit with Cupid's archery,
 Sink in apple of his eye.
 When his love he doth espy,   105
 Let her shine as gloriously
 As the Venus of the sky.
 When thou wak'st, if she be by,
 Beg of her for remedy.

quite – *completely*

misprision – *mistaking*; perforce – *forcibly*; ensue – *result in*
turn'd – *changed/ made unfaithful*

o'er-rules – *has taken charge*; one . . . troth – *for every man keeping faith*
confounding oath on oath – *breaking one oath after another*

fancy-sick – *love-sick*; cheer – *complexion*
that . . . dear – *(each sigh was thought to cost a drop of blood)*
illusion – *deception*
against – *ready for when*; do – *does*   Qq – do F – doth

                                                    Metre – this line is short by 2 syl.
Tartar – *savage inhabitant of Asia Minor*

            Metre – catalectic trochaic tetrameter – see Introduction – Magic Metre
Hit . . . archery – *Hit by Cupid's arrow* (see 2.1.165)
apple – *the pupil*
espy – *see*
gloriously – *brightly*
Venus – (see Myth)

remedy – *relief*

Enter PUCK.

PUCK

    Captain of our fairy band,   110
    Helena is here at hand;
    And the youth, mistook by me,
    Pleading for a lover's fee.
    Shall we their fond pageant see?
    Lord, what fools these mortals be!   115

OBERON

    Stand aside. The noise they make
    Will cause Demetrius to awake.

PUCK

    Then will two at once woo one:
    That must needs be sport alone;
    And those things do best please me   120
    That befall prepost'rously.

[They stand aside.]
Enter LYSANDER *and* HELENA.

LYSANDER

    Why should you think that I should woo in scorn?
    Scorn and derision never come in tears.
    Look when I vow, I weep; and vows so born,
    In their nativity all truth appears.   125
    How can these things in me seem scorn to you,
    Bearing the badge of faith to prove them true?

HELENA

    You do advance your cunning more and more.
    When truth kills truth, O devilish-holy fray!

mistook – *mistaken*
fee – *payment*
fond pageant – *foolish spectacle*
be – *are*

alone – *it itself*

befall – *fall out*; prepost'rously – *out of the natural course*

Look . . . appears – *The fact that I am weeping indicates the truth of my vows*

badge – *sign (his tears)*

advance – *increase*
truth kills truth – *the truth of one vow (to Helena) nullifies that of the other (to Hermia)*;
delivish-holy – *both diabolical and sanctified*   **dev**-ilish (equiv. 2 syl.)

These vows are Hermia's: will you give her o'er?   130
Weigh oath with oath, and you will nothing weigh:
Your vows to her and me, put in two scales,
Will even weigh; and both as light as tales.

LYSANDER

I had no judgement when to her I swore.

HELENA

Nor none, in my mind, now you give her o'er.   135

LYSANDER

Demetrius loves her, and he loves not you.

DEMETRIUS

[*waking*] O Helen, goddess, nymph, perfect, divine!
To what, my love, shall I compare thine eyne?
Crystal is muddy. O how ripe in show
Thy lips, those kissing cherries, tempting grow!   140
That pure congealèd white, high Taurus' snow,
Fann'd with the eastern wind, turns to a crow
When thou hold'st up thy hand. O let me kiss
This princess of pure white, this seal of bliss!

HELENA

O spite! O hell! I see you all are bent   145
To set against me for your merriment.
If you were civil, and knew courtesy,
You would not do me thus much injury.
Can you not hate me, as I know you do,
But you must join in souls to mock me too?   150
If you were men, as men you are in show,
You would not use a gentle lady so:
To vow, and swear, and superpraise my parts,

o'er – *up*

weigh . . . weigh – *weigh one oath against another and they will weigh nothing*

tales – *idle rumours*

o'er – *up*

Rhyme – this line is outside the rhyme scheme

eyne – *eyes*

ripe – *red and full*; show – *appearance*

congealèd – *solid*; Taurus – *mountain range in Asia Minor*

turns to a crow – *looks black in comparison*

seal – *promise*

bent – *determined to*   Qq – all are F – are all

set against – *set upon*

do . . . injury – *insult me so*

join in souls – *unite*

show – *appearance*   Qq – were F – are

use – *treat*; gentle – *well born/ mild*

superpraise – *praise excessively*; parts – *qualities*

When I am sure you hate me with your hearts.
You both are rivals, and love Hermia;   155
And now both rivals to mock Helena.
A trim exploit, a manly enterprise,
To conjure tears up in a poor maid's eyes
With your derision! None of noble sort
Would so offend a virgin, and extort   160
A poor soul's patience, all to make you sport.

LYSANDER
You are unkind, Demetrius; be not so,
For you love Hermia; this you know I know:
And here, with all good will, with all my heart,
In Hermia's love I yield you up my part;   165
And yours of Helena to me bequeath,
Whom I do love, and will do till my death.

HELENA
Never did mockers waste more idle breath.

DEMETRIUS
Lysander, keep thy Hermia; I will none.
If ere I lov'd her, all that love is gone.   170
My heart to her but as guest-wise sojourn'd,
And now to Helen is it home return'd,
There to remain.

LYSANDER   Helen, it is not so.

DEMETRIUS
Disparage not the faith thou dost not know,
Lest to thy peril thou aby it dear.   175
Look where thy love comes; yonder is thy dear.

trim – *fine*; exploit – *deed*
conjure tears up – *make tears appear by magic*
sort – *rank*
extort – *torture*

yield you up – *give to you*
to me bequeath – *bequeath to me*

Q1 – till Q2/F – to

I will none – *want nothing to do with her*
ere – *ever/ before*
but . . . sojourn'd – *stayed only as a guest*

Q1 – is it Q2/F – it is

Disparage not – *don't undervalue*
aby it dear – *suffer for it dearly*

Q1 – aby Q2/F – abide

Enter HERMIA.

HERMIA

    Dark night, that from the eye his function takes,
    The ear more quick of apprehension makes;
    Wherein it doth impair the seeing sense,
    It pays the hearing double recompense.   180
    Thou art not by mine eye, Lysander, found;
    Mine ear, I thank it, brought me to thy sound.
    But why unkindly didst thou leave me so?

LYSANDER

    Why should he stay whom love doth press to go?

HERMIA

    What love could press Lysander from my side?   185

LYSANDER

    Lysander's love, that would not let him bide –
    Fair Helena, who more engilds the night
    Than all yon fiery oes and eyes of light.
    Why seek'st thou me? Could not this make thee know
    The hate I bare thee made me leave thee so?   190

HERMIA

    You speak not as you think; it cannot be!

HELENA

    Lo, she is one of this confederacy!
    Now I perceive they have conjoin'd all three
    To fashion this false sport in spite of me.
    Injurious Hermia! Most ungrateful maid!   195
    Have you conspir'd, have you with these contriv'd,
    To bait me with this foul derision?

his – *its*
apprehension – *perception*
Wherein – *In that*

Qq – thy F – that

press – *urge*

bide – *remain*
engilds – *brightens with gold*
yon – *over there*; oes and eyes of light – *stars*

Lo – *Oh*; confederacy – *alliance*   con-**fed**-er-**acy** (equiv. 4 syl.)
conjoin'd – *joined up*
fashion – *contrive*; in spite of – *to spite*
Injurious – *Harmful*   In-**ju**-rious (equiv. 3 syl)
          Rhyme – the dialogue moves out of rhyme
bait – *torment*; derision – *ridicule*   de-**ris**-i-**on** (equiv. 4 syl.)

Is all the counsel that we two have shar'd,
The sisters' vows, the hours that we have spent
When we have chid the hasty-footed time   200
For parting us – O, is all forgot?
All school-days' friendship, childhood innocence?
We, Hermia, like two artificial gods,
Have with our needles created both one flower,
Both on one sampler, sitting on one cushion,   205
Both warbling of one song, both in one key,
As if our hands, our sides, voices and minds,
Had been incorporate. So we grew together,
Like to a double cherry, seeming parted,
But yet an union in partition,   210
Two lovely berries moulded on one stem;
So, with two seeming bodies, but one heart;
Two of the first, like coats in heraldry,
Due but to one, and crownèd with one crest.
And will you rent our ancient love asunder   215
To join with men in scorning your poor friend?
It is not friendly, 'tis not maidenly;
Our sex, as well as I, may chide you for it,
Though I alone do feel the injury.

HERMIA

I am amazèd at your passionate words: 220
I scorn you not; it seems that you scorn me.

HELENA

Have you not set Lysander, as in scorn,
To follow me, and praise my eyes and face;
And made your other love, Demetrius,
Who even but now did spurn me with his foot,   225
To call me goddess, nymph, divine and rare,

counsel – *confidences*

chid – *scolded*

> Metre – the line is short by 1 syl. (possibly at the caesural break – see 'A Note on Metre')

artificial – *skilled in the art of creation*

> needles (equiv. 1 syl.)

sampler – *piece of embroidery*

sides – *bodies*
incorporate – *of one body*
Like to – *Similar to*

> Qq – an F – a

two seeming bodies – *the appearance of two bodies*
of the first – *bodies/first colour on a heraldic shield*; coats – *coats of arms*
Due but to one – *Owned by a single person*
rent – *tear*; ancient – *long-standing*; asunder – *apart*

chide – *scold*

> **pass**-ionate (equiv. 2 syl.)

even but now – *just now*; spurn – *kick*

> even (equiv. 1 syl.)

Precious, celestial? Wherefore speaks he this
To her he hates? And wherefore doth Lysander
Deny your love, so rich within his soul,
And tender me, forsooth, affection,   230
But by your setting on, by your consent?
What though I be not so in grace as you,
So hung upon with love, so fortunate,
But miserable most, to love unlov'd?
This you should pity rather than despise.   235

HERMIA
I understand not what you mean by this.

HELENA
Ay, do! Persever: counterfeit sad looks,
Make mouths upon me when I turn my back,
Wink each at other; hold the sweet jest up;
This sport, well carried, shall be chronicl'd.   240
If you have any pity, grace, or manners,
You would not make me such an argument.
But fare ye well; 'tis partly my own fault,
Which death, or absence, soon shall remedy.

LYSANDER
Stay, gentle Helena; hear my excuse;   245
My love, my life, my soul, fair Helena!

HELENA
O excellent!

HERMIA   Sweet, do not scorn her so.

DEMETRIUS
If she cannot entreat, I can compel.

celestial – *heavenly*; Wherefore – *Why*   ce-**les**-tial (equiv. 3 syl.)

tender – *offer*; forsooth – *in truth*
But – *except*; setting on – *encouragement*
What though – *What if*; grace – *favour*

Persever – *Persevere*; sad – *serious*   Persever – Pron. – Per-**sev**-er
mouths – *faces*
hold . . . up – *keep up the joke*
carried – *managed*; chronicl'd – *recorded in history*

argument – *subject for a joke*

Q1 – my Q2/F – mine

(To Lysander) If . . . compel – *If she can't entreat you to stop, I can make you*

LYSANDER

    Thou canst compel no more than she entreat;

    Thy threats have no more strength than her weak prayers.   250

    Helen, I love thee, by my life I do;

    I swear by that which I will lose for thee

    To prove him false that says I love thee not.

DEMETRIUS

    I say I love thee more than he can do.

LYSANDER

    If thou say so, withdraw and prove it too.   255

DEMETRIUS

    Quick, come!

HERMIA   Lysander, whereto tends all this?

LYSANDER

    Away, you Ethiope!

DEMETRIUS   No, no; he'll

    Seem to break loose – [*to Lysander*] take on as you
       would follow,

    But yet come not! You are a tame man, go!

LYSANDER

    Hang off, thou cat, thou burr! Vile thing, let loose,   260

    Or I will shake thee from me like a serpent.

HERMIA

    Why are you grown so rude? What change is this,

    Sweet love?

withdraw – *come with me*

whereto . . . this? – *what does his mean?*

Ethiope – *Ethiopian*   Metre – as a shared line this is short by 1 syl.
(possibly at the mid-line caesura. See 'A Note on Metre'.)

Seem – *Pretend*; break loose – *(from Hermia)*; take on – *behave as if*

tame – *weak*

burr – *sticky fruiting head of the burdock*

rude – *rough*

LYSANDER   Thy love? Out, tawny Tartar, out!
　　Out, loathèd medicine! O hated potion, hence!

HERMIA
　　Do you not jest?

HELENA   Yes sooth, and so do you.   265

LYSANDER
　　Demetrius, I will keep my word with thee.

DEMETRIUS
　　I would I had your bond, for I perceive
　　A weak bond holds you; I'll not trust your word.

LYSANDER
　　What, should I hurt her, strike her, kill her dead?
　　Although I hate her, I'll not harm her so.   270

HERMIA
　　What, can you do me greater harm than hate?
　　Hate me? Wherefor? O me! what news, my love?
　　Am not I Hermia? Are not you Lysander?
　　I am as fair now as I was erewhile.
　　Since night you lov'd me; yet since night you left me   275
　　Why, then you left me – O the gods forbid! –
　　In earnest, shall I say?

LYSANDER   Ay, by my life!
　　And never did desire to see thee more.
　　Therefore, be out of hope, of question, of doubt;
　　Be certain, nothing truer; 'tis no jest   280
　　That I do hate thee, and love Helena.

Out – *Get away*; tawny – *tan-coloured*; Tartar – *person from central Asia*

Irregular line (see Introduction); Q1 – potion Q2/F – poison

sooth – *truly*

bond – *contract/tie*

weak bond – *(i.e. Hermia)*

Wherefor? – *Why?*   Wherefor? – Pron. – Where-**for?**

erewhile – *before*

be out of – *abandon*   -tion, of **doubt** (anapest); Qq/F – of doubt Pope – doubt

HERMIA

    O me! [*to Helena*] You juggler! You canker-blossom!
    You thief of love! What, have you come by night
    And stol'n my love's heart from him?

HELENA   Fine, i'faith!
    Have you no modesty, no maiden shame,   285
    No touch of bashfulness? What, will you tear
    Impatient answers from my gentle tongue?
    Fie, fie, you counterfeit! You puppet you!

HERMIA

    'Puppet'! Why, so? Ay, that way goes the game!
    Now I perceive that she hath made compare   290
    Between our statures; she hath urg'd her height;
    And with her personage, her tall personage,
    Her height, forsooth, she hath prevail'd with him.
    And are you grown so high in his esteem
    Because I am so dwarfish and so low?   295
    How low am I, thou painted maypole? Speak:
    How low am I? I am not yet so low
    But that my nails can reach unto thine eyes.

HELENA

    I pray you, though you mock me, gentlemen,
    Let her not hurt me. I was never curst;   300
    I have no gift at all in shrewishness;
    I am a right maid for my cowardice;
    Let her not strike me. You perhaps may think,
    Because she is something lower than myself,
    That I can match her.

juggler (**ju**-gg-**ler**) – *trickster*; canker-blossom – *grub that ruins blossoms (of love)*

Impatient – *angry*
counterfeit – *fake*; puppet – *false/ small thing*

Why, so? – *O, indeed*

urg'd – *insisted on*
personage – *appearance*   **pers**-onage (equiv. 2 syl.)
prevail'd with him – *succeeded in achieving him*

painted maypole – *(insult suggesting she is over-made-up and skinny).*

curst – *bad tempered*

right – *proper*; for – *in*

something lower – *somewhat shorter*   she is **some**- (anapest – see 'A Note on Metre')
can match – *am a match for*

HERMIA   'Lower'? Hark, again!   305

HELENA
   Good Hermia, do not be so bitter with me.
   I evermore did love you, Hermia,
   Did ever keep your counsels, never wrong'd you,
   Save that, in love unto Demetrius,
   I told him of your stealth unto this wood.   310
   He follow'd you; for love I follow'd him;
   But he hath chid me hence, and threaten'd me
   To strike me, spurn me, nay, to kill me too:
   And now, so you will let me quiet go,
   To Athens will I bear my folly back,   315
   And follow you no further. Let me go:
   You see how simple and how fond I am.

HERMIA
   Why, get you gone! Who is't that hinders you?

HELENA
   A foolish heart that I leave here behind.

HERMIA
   What! with Lysander?

HELENA   With Demetrius.   320

LYSANDER
   Be not afraid; she shall not harm thee, Helena.

DEMETRIUS
   No sir, she shall not, though you take her part.

evermore – *always*
counsels – *secrets*
Save – *Except*
stealth – *stealing away*

chid me hence – *tried to drive me away by scolding*
spurn – *kick*
so – *if*

fond – *foolish*

hinders – *prevents*

part – *side*

HELENA
O, when she is angry, she is keen and shrewd;
She was a vixen when she went to school,
And though she be but little, she is fierce.   325

HERMIA
'Little' again? Nothing but 'low' and 'little'?
Why will you suffer her to flout me thus?
Let me come to her!

LYSANDER   Get you gone, you dwarf;
You minimus, of hindering knot-grass made;
You bead, you acorn.

DEMETRIUS   You are too officious   330
In her behalf that scorns your services.
Let her alone; speak not of Helena;
Take not her part; for if thou dost intend
Never so little show of love to her.
Thou shall aby it.

LYSANDER   Now she holds me not: 335
Now follow, if thou dar'st, to try whose right,
Of thine or mine, is most in Helena.

DEMETRIUS
Follow? Nay, I'll go with thee, cheek by jowl.

Exeunt Lysander and Demetrius.

HERMIA
You, mistress, all this coil is long of you.
Nay, go not back.

keen – *sharp*; shrewd – *malicious*   she is **an-** (anapest); Q1 – she is Q2/F – she's
vixen – *female fox*

suffer – *allow*; flout – *mock*

minimus – *insignificant thing*; knot-grass – *creeping weed*

officious – *dutiful*
In – *On*

part – *side*

aby – *pay dearly for*   Qq – aby F – abide

Of – *out of*

cheek by jowl – *cheek to cheek* (Prov.)

coil – *fuss*; long – *because*

HELENA   I will not trust you, I,   340
     Nor longer stay in your curst company.
     Your hands than mine are quicker for a fray:
     My legs are longer though, to run away.

                          Exit.

HERMIA
     I am amaz'd, and know not what to say.

                          Exit.

[*Oberon and Puck come forward.*]

OBERON
     This is thy negligence: still thou mistak'st,   345
     Or else committ'st thy knaveries wilfully.

PUCK
     Believe me, king of shadows, I mistook.
     Did not you tell me I should know the man
     By the Athenian garments he had on?
     And so far blameless proves my enterprise   350
     That I have 'nointed an Athenian's eyes:
     And so far am I glad it so did sort,
     As this their jangling I esteem a sport.

OBERON
     Thou seest these lovers seek a place to fight.
     Hie therefore, Robin, overcast the night;   355
     The starry welkin cover thou anon
     With drooping fog, as black as Acheron,

fray – *attack*

knaveries – *boyish tricks*; wilfully – *on purpose*   **kna**-veries (equiv. 2 syl.);
                                                            Qq – wilfully F – willingly

shadows – *spirits*

                                                            Q1 – had Q2/F – hath
                                    Rhyme – the scene moves back into rhyming couplets
'nointed – *anointed/ smeared*
sort – *turn out*
jangling – *arguing*; esteem – *regard as*

Hie – *Hasten*
welkin – *sky*; anon – *instantly*
Acheron (**A**-ke-**ron**) – *the river of woe (one of the rivers of the underworld)*

And lead these testy rivals so astray
As one come not within another's way.
Like to Lysander sometime frame thy tongue,   360
Then stir Demetrius up with bitter wrong;
And sometime rail thou like Demetrius:
And from each other look thou lead them thus,
Till o'er their brows death-counterfeiting sleep
With leaden legs and batty wings doth creep.   365
Then crush this herb into Lysander's eye,
Whose liquor hath this virtuous property,
To take from thence all error with his might,
And make his eyeballs roll with wonted sight.
When they next wake, all this derision   370
Shall seem a dream and fruitless vision;
And back to Athens shall the lovers wend,
With league whose date till death shall never end.
Whiles I in this affair do thee employ,
I'll to my queen, and beg her Indian boy;   375
And then I will her charmèd eye release
From monster's view, and all things shall be peace.

PUCK

My fairy lord, this must be done with haste,
For night's swift dragons cut the clouds full fast;
And yonder shines Aurora's harbinger,   380
At whose approach, ghosts wandering here and there
Troop home to churchyards. Damnèd spirits all,
That in cross-ways and floods have burial,
Already to their wormy beds are gone,
For fear lest day should look their shames upon: 385
They wilfully themselves exil'd from light,

testy – *irritable*
As – *So that*
Like ... tongue – *Sometimes imitate Lysander's voice*
wrong – *insults*
rail – *rant*

o'er – *over*; death-counterfeiting sleep – *sleep that seems like death* (Prov.)
leaden – *heavy*; batty – *bat-like*

liquor – *juice*; virtuous – *powerful*   **vir**-tuous (equiv. 2 syl.)
his – *its*
wonted – *accustomed*
derision – *ridiculousness*   Metre suggests der-**i**-si-**on** (equiv. 4 syl.)
fruitless – *pointless*   Metre suggests **vis**-i-**on** (equiv. 3 syl.)
wend – *make their way*
league – *friendship*; whose ... end – *that will last until death*

night's swift dragons – *(drawing the chariot of night)*
Aurora's harbinger – *the morning star (announcing the arrival of the dawn)* (see Myth)

Damnèd spirits – *those who killed themselves (not permitted Christian burial)*
cross-ways – *crossroads (where suicides were buried)*; floods – *(those who drowned themselves)*
look ... upon – *look upon their shame*
wilfully ... light – *(by committing suicide)*   Alexander – exil'd Qq – exile

And must for aye consort with black-brow'd night.

OBERON
But we are spirits of another sort:
I with the Morning's love have oft made sport;
And like a forester the groves may tread   390
Even till the eastern gate, all fiery-red,
Opening on Neptune with fair blessèd beams,
Turns into yellow gold his salt green streams.
But notwithstanding, haste, make no delay;
We may effect this business yet ere day.   395

[Exit]

PUCK
Up and down, up and down,
I will lead them up and down;
I am fear'd in field and town:
Goblin, lead them up and down.
Here comes one.   400

Enter LYSANDER.

LYSANDER
Where art thou, proud Demetrius? Speak thou now.

PUCK
Here, villain, drawn and ready. Where art thou?

LYSANDER
I will be with thee straight.

PUCK   Follow me then

for aye – *for ever*, consort – *keep company*

I ... sport – *I have often dallied with Morning (the goddess Aurora)* (see Myth)
forester – *guardian of the forest*
eastern gate – *(where the sun rises)*   Even (equiv. 1 syl.)
Opening – *Rising*; Neptune – (see Myth)

notwithstanding – *nevertheless*

Metre – this rhyme is in catalectic trochaic tetrameter – see Introduction – Magic Metre.
                 This line is missing a beat at the caesura – see 'A Note on Metre'.

Goblin – *(referring to himself)*

drawn – *with sword drawn*

straight – *straight away*

To plainer ground.

[Exit Lysander, as following the voice.]
Enter DEMETRIUS.

DEMETRIUS   Lysander, speak again.
Thou runaway, thou coward, art thou fled?   405
Speak! In some bush? Where dost thou hide thy head?

PUCK
Thou coward, art thou bragging to the stars,
Telling the bushes that thou look'st for wars,
And wilt not come? Come, recreant, come thou child!
I'll whip thee with a rod; he is defil'd   410
That draws a sword on thee.

DEMETRIUS   Yea, art thou there?

PUCK
Follow my voice; we'll try no manhood here

Exeunt.

[Enter LYSANDER.*]*

LYSANDER
He goes before me, and still dares me on;
When I come where he calls, then he is gone.
The villain is much lighter-heel'd than I: 415
I follow'd fast; but faster he did fly,
That fallen am I in dark uneven way,
And here will rest me.

Lies down.

plainer – *more open*

In ... bush – *Are you in a bush?*

bragging – *boasting*

recreant – *coward*   **re**-creant (equiv. 2 syl.)
rod – *cane*; defil'd – *sullied*

try – *test*

fallen ... in – *I got into*   fallen (equiv. 1 syl.)

> Come thou gentle day:
For if but once thou show me thy grey light,
I'll find Demetrius, and revenge this spite.   [*Sleeps.*]   420

Enter PUCK *and* DEMETRIUS.

PUCK
Ho, ho, ho! Coward, why com'st thou not?

[*They dodge about the stage.*]

DEMETRIUS
Abide me if thou dar'st, for well I wot
Thou runn'st before me, shifting every place,
And dar'st not stand, nor look me in the face.
Where art thou now?

PUCK   Come hither; I am here.   425

DEMETRIUS
Nay, then, thou mock'st me; thou shalt buy this dear
If ever I thy face by daylight see:
Now go thy way. Faintness constraineth me
To measure out my length on this cold bed.
    [*Lies down.*]
By day's approach look to be visited.   [*Sleeps.*]   430

Enter HELENA.

HELENA
O weary night, O long and tedious night,
Abate thy hours! Shine, comforts, from the east,
That I may back to Athens by daylight,
From these that my poor company detest.

spite – *bad turn*

Metre – line is headless (see 'A Note on Metre')

Abide – *Confront*; wot – *know*

stand – *wait/attack*

buy – *pay for*

constraineth – *compels*
measure out my length – *lie down*

te-dious (equiv. 2 syl.); Rhyme – four alternate rhyming lines
Abate thy hours – *make your hours seem shorter*

'detest' would, presumably, have rhymed with 'east'

And sleep, that sometimes shuts up sorrow's eye,   435
Steal me awhile from mine own company.

[Lies down and] sleeps.

PUCK
   Yet but three? Come one more,
   Two of both kinds makes up four.
   Here she comes, curst and sad:
   Cupid is a knavish lad   440
   Thus to make poor females mad!

Enter HERMIA.

HERMIA
   Never so weary, never so in woe,
   Bedabbled with the dew, and torn with briars,
   I can no further crawl, no further go;
   My legs can keep no pace with my desires.   445
   Here will I rest me till the break of day.   *[Lies down.]*
   Heavens shield Lysander, if they mean a fray! *[Sleeps.]*

PUCK
   On the ground
   Sleep sound;
   I'll apply   450
   To your eye,
   Gentle lover, remedy.

[Squeezes the juice on Lysander's eyelids.]

When thou wak'st,
Thou tak'st

Qq – sometimes F – sometime

Steal – *Keep*

Metre – catalectic trochaic tetrameter – see Introduction – Magic Metre.
This line is missing a beat at the caesura – see 'A Note on Metre'.

curst – *ill-tempered*   This line is missing a beat at the caesura

Rhyme – four alternate rhyming lines

Bedabbled – *Wet*

fray – *attack*   Heavens (equiv. 1 syl.)

Metre – see Introduction – Magic Metre

True delight   455
In the sight
Of thy former lady's eye;
And the country proverb known,
That every man should take his own,
In your waking shall be shown: 460
Jack shall have Jill,
Nought shall go ill;
The man shall have his mare again, and all shall be well.

[Exit.]

ACT 4, SCENE 1

Lysander, Demetrius, Helena and Hermia, still lying asleep. Enter
TITANIA, *Queen of Fairies, and* BOTTOM; PEASEBLOSSOM,
COBWEB, MOTH, MUSTARDSEED *and other fairies;* OBERON, *the*
King, behind, [unseen.]

TITANIA
Come sit thee down upon this flowery bed,
While I thy amiable cheeks do coy,
And stick musk-roses in thy sleek smooth head,
And kiss thy fair large ears, my gentle joy.

BOTTOM
Where's Peaseblossom?   5

PEASEBLOSSOM
Ready.

BOTTOM
Scratch my head, Peaseblossom. Where's Mounsieur
Cobweb?

Jack shall have Jill – Prov.

Nought – *Nothing*

man ... mare again – Prov.

Rhyme – alternate rhyming lines. Titania speaks in VERSE and Bottom in PROSE.

amiable – *lovable*; coy – *caress*

COBWEB
Ready.

BOTTOM
Mounsieur Cobweb, good mounsieur, get you your 10
weapons in your hand, and kill me a red-hipped
humble-bee on the top of a thistle; and good
mounsieur, bring me the honey-bag. Do not fret
yourself too much in the action, mounsieur; and
good mounsieur, have a care the honey-bag break 15
not; I would be loath to have you overflowen with
a honey-bag, signior. Where's Mounsieur
Mustardseed?

MUSTARDSEED
Ready.

BOTTOM
Give me your neaf, Mounsieur Mustardseed. Pray 20
you, leave your courtesy, good mounsieur.

MUSTARDSEED
What's your will?

BOTTOM
Nothing, good mounsieur, but to help Cavalery
Cobweb to scratch. I must to the barber's, mounsieur,
for methinks I am marvellous hairy about the 25
face; and I am such a tender ass, if my hair do but
tickle me, I must scratch.

TITANIA
What, wilt thou hear some music, my sweet love?

Q1 – you your Q2/F – your

humble-bee – *bumble bee*

overflowen – *flowed over*

neaf – *fist*

leave your courtesy – *do not stand bareheaded/*   Q2/F – courtesy Q1 – curtsie
stop bowing

Cavalery – *cavelier (a sprightly military man)*

marvellous – *extremely*

BOTTOM

I have a reasonable good ear in music. Let's have
the tongs and the bones.   30

TITANIA

Or say, sweet love, what thou desir'st to eat?

BOTTOM

Truly, a peck of provender; I could munch your
good dry oats. Methinks I have a great desire to a
bottle of hay: good hay, sweet hay, hath no fellow.

TITANIA

I have a venturous fairy that shall seek   35
The squirrel's hoard, and fetch thee new nuts.

BOTTOM

I had rather have a handful or two of dried peas.
But I pray you, let none of your people stir me:
I have an exposition of sleep come upon me.

TITANIA

Sleep thou, and I will wind thee in my arms.   40
Fairies, be gone, and be all ways away.

[Exeunt Fairies.]

So doth the woodbine the sweet honeysuckle
Gently entwist; the female ivy so
Enrings the barky fingers of the elm.
O how I love thee! How I dote on thee! [*They sleep.*]   45

Enter PUCK

Q1 – Let's Q2/F – Let us

tongs and the bones – *percussion instruments*

peck of provender – *quantity of fodder*

bottle – *bundle*; hath no fellow – *there's nothing like it*

venturous – *adventurous*
      Metre – this line is short by 1 syl. (new may have been pronounced as 2 syl.
           – **knee**-oo)

stir me – *wake me*
exposition of – *malapropism for disposition to*

all ways – *in every direction*   Theobald – all ways Qq/F – always

So – *Thus*; the woodbine – *a climbing plant (possibly Virginia Creeper)*

Enrings – *Encircles*; barky fingers – *branches*
dote on – *love*

OBERON

    [*advancing*]

    Welcome, good Robin. Seest thou this sweet sight.

    Her dotage now I do begin to pity;

    For, meeting her of late behind the wood

    Seeking sweet favours for this hateful fool,

    I did upbraid her and fall out with her: 50

    For she his hairy temples then had rounded

    With coronet of fresh and fragrant flowers;

    And that same dew, which sometime on the buds

    Was wont to swell like round and orient pearls,

    Stood now within the pretty flowerets' eyes   55

    Like tears, that did their own disgrace bewail.

    When I had at my pleasure taunted her,

    And she in mild terms begg'd my patience,

    I then did ask of her her changeling child;

    Which straight she gave me, and her fairy sent   60

    To bear him to my bower in fairy land.

    And now I have the boy, I will undo

    This hateful imperfection of her eyes.

    And gentle Puck, take this transformèd scalp

    From off the head of this Athenian swain,   65

    That he awaking when the other do,

    May all to Athens back again repair,

    And think no more of this night's accidents

    But as the fierce vexation of a dream.

    But first I will release the fairy queen.   70

        [Squeezes the juice on her eyelids.]

    Be as thou wast wont to be;

    See as thou wont to see:

    Dian's bud o'er Cupid's flower

dotage – *infatuation*

favours – *love tokens*   Q1 – favours Q2/f – savours
upbraid – *find fault with*

coronet – *crown*
sometime – *formerly*
wont – *accustomed*; orient – *Eastern*
flowerets – *small flowers*

Metre suggests **pa**-ti-**ence** (equiv. 3 syl.)

straight – *straight away*

swain – *rustic*
the other – *the others (the lovers)*
repair – *return*
accidents – *events*
vexation – *distress*

wont – *accustomed*   Metre – spell is in catalectic trochaic tetrameter – see
                                                            Intro. – Magic Metre
Dian's bud – *the herb antidote (possibly onions or chaste tree)*; o'er – *over*

Hath such force and blessèd power.
Now my Titania, wake you, my sweet queen.   75

TITANIA
[*waking*] My Oberon! What visions have I seen!
Methought I was enamour'd of an ass.

OBERON
There lies your love.

TITANIA   How came these things to pass?
O how mine eyes do loathe his visage now!

OBERON
Silence awhile. Robin, take off this head.   80
Titania, music call; and strike more dead
Than common sleep, of all these five the sense.

TITANIA
Music ho, music, such as charmeth sleep!

[Soft music.]

PUCK
[*taking the ass-head off Bottom*]
Now when thou wak'st, with thine own fool's eyes peep.

OBERON
Sound, music!   *[Music strikes into a dance.]*
                    Come my queen, take hands with me,   85
And rock the ground whereon these sleepers be.

[Oberon and Titania dance.]

enamour'd of – *in love with*

visage – *face*

Qq – this F – his

of all these five – *the four lovers and Bottom*; sense – *senses*

charmeth – *brings about by magic*

peep – *see*

Q1 – Now when Q2/F – When

Rhyme – rhyming couplets

Now thou and I are new in amity,
And will to-morrow midnight, solemnly,
Dance in Duke Theseus' house triumphantly,
And bless it to all fair prosperity.   90
There shall the pairs of faithful lovers be
Wedded, with Theseus, all in jollity.

PUCK

Fairy king, attend and mark:
I do hear the morning lark.

OBERON

Then my queen, in silence sad,   95
Trip we after night's shade:
We the globe can compass soon,
Swifter than the wandering moon.

TITANIA

Come my lord, and in our flight
Tell me how it came this night   100
That I sleeping here was found
With these mortals on the ground.

Exeunt. The four lovers and Bottom still lie asleep.
To the winding of horns within, enter THESEUS,
HIPPOLYTA, EGEUS and train.

THESEUS

Go one of you, find out the forester;
For now our observation is perform'd,
And since we have the vaward of the day,   105
My love shall hear the music of my hounds.

amity – *friendship*
solemnly – *in festive ritual*
triumphantly – *in festive triumph*
prosperity – *wealth and success* Q1 – prosperity Q2/F – posterity

attend – *listen*; mark – *take notice* Metre – catalectic trochaic tetrameter – see
Intro. – Magic Metre

silence sad – *sober silence*
Trip – *move swiftly* Metre suggests **nigh**-tes (2 syl.); Q1 – night's
compass – *orbit* Q2/F – the night's

forester – *officer of the forest*
observation – *observance (to the morn of May)*
vaward – *earliest part* vaward – Pron. – **vow**-ward

Uncouple in the western valley; let them go;
Dispatch I say, and find the forester.

Exit an attendant.

We will, fair queen, up to the mountain's top,
And mark the musical confusion   110
Of hounds and echo in conjunction.

HIPPOLYTA
I was with Hercules and Cadmus once,
When in a wood of Crete they bay'd the bear
With hounds of Sparta; never did I hear
Such gallant chiding; for, besides the groves,   115
The skies, the fountains, every region near
Seem'd all one mutual cry; I never heard
So musical a discord, such sweet thunder.

THESEUS
My hounds are bred out of the Spartan kind,
So flew'd, so sanded; and their heads are hung   120
With ears that sweep away the morning dew;
Crook-knee'd and dewlapp'd like Thessalian bulls;
Slow in pursuit, but match'd in mouth like bells,
Each under each: a cry more tuneable
Was never holla'd to, nor cheer'd with horn,   125
In Crete, in Sparta, nor in Thessaly.
Judge when you hear. But soft, what nymphs are these?

EGEUS
My lord, this is my daughter here asleep,
And this Lysander; this Demetrius is,

Uncouple – *Release them*   Irregular line – can be scanned with quartus paeon
                                                      (see 'A Note on Metre')

Metre suggests con-**fus**-i-**on** (equiv. 4 syl.)
Metre suggests con-**junc**-ti-**on** (equiv. 4 syl.)

Hercules . . . Cadmus (see Myth)

bay'd – *pursued with hounds*
hounds of Sparta – *(famous as hunting dogs)*; Sparta – *a city state in Ancient Greece*
çhiding – *barking*

mutual – *common*

kind – *breed*
flew'd – *with large chaps*; sanded – *sandy-coloured*

dewlapp'd – *with folds of skin at the throat*   Pron. – Thess-**ay**-lian
match'd . . . Each – *matched in the pitch of their barking, like bells in harmony*
cry – *pack of hounds*; tuneable – *melodious*
holla'd – *shouted ('halloo')*; cheer'd – *urged on*
Thessaly – *area of Ancient Greece otherwise known as Aeolia*
soft – *stop*

This Helena, old Nedar's Helena.   130
I wonder of their being here together.

THESEUS
No doubt they rose up early, to observe
The rite of May; and hearing our intent,
Came here in grace of our solemnity.
But speak, Egeus; is not this the day   135
That Hermia should give answer of her choice?

EGEUS
It is, my lord.

THESEUS
Go, bid the huntsmen wake them with their horns.

[Shout within; winding of horns.]
[The lovers wake and start up.]

Good-morrow friends. Saint Valentine is past:
Begin these wood-birds but to couple now?   140

LYSANDER
Pardon, my lord.

[The lovers kneel.]

THESEUS   I pray you all, stand up.
I know you two are rival enemies:
How comes this gentle concord in the world,
That hatred is so far from jealousy
To sleep by hate, and fear no enmity?   145

Nedar – Pron. – **Nay**-dar
of – *at*   Q1 – their Q2/F – this

rite of May – *celebrations for May Day (1 May)*
in grace of – *to honour*; solemnity – *ceremony*

Metre – line is short by 6 syl.

Saint Valentine – *Valentine's Day, the festival on which birds were supposed to couple*
but to – *to only*

concord – *agreement*
jealousy – *suspicion*
enmity – *hostility*

LYSANDER

    My lord, I shall reply amazedly,
    Half sleep, half waking; but as yet, I swear,
    I cannot truly say how I came here.
    But as I think – for truly would I speak –
    And now I do bethink me, so it is: 150
    I came with Hermia hither; our intent
    Was to be gone from Athens, where we might,
    Without the peril of the Athenian law –

EGEUS

    Enough, enough, my lord; you have enough!
    I beg the law, the law upon his head!   155
    They would have stol'n away, they would, Demetrius,
    Thereby to have defeated you and me:
    You of your wife, and me of my consent,
    Of my consent that she should be your wife.

DEMETRIUS

    My lord, fair Helen told me of their stealth,   160
    Of this their purpose hither to this wood;
    And I in fury hither follow'd them,
    Fair Helena in fancy following me.
    But my good lord, I wot not by what power –
    But by some power it is – my love to Hermia,   165
    Melted as the snow, seems to me now
    As the remembrance of an idle gaud
    Which in my childhood I did dote upon;
    And all the faith, the virtue of my heart,
    The object and the pleasure of mine eye,   170
    Is only Helena. To her, my lord,
    Was I betroth'd ere I saw Hermia;
    But like a sickness did I loathe this food:
    But as in health, come to my natural taste,

amazedly – *confusedly*

hither – *to this place*

Without – *Out of reach of*

defeated – *defrauded*

hither – *in coming here*

in fancy – *out of love*   **foll**-owing (equiv. 2 syl.); Q1 – following Q2/F – followed
wot – *know*

Metre – line is headless (see 'A Note on Metre')
As – *Like*; idle gaud – *worthless trinket*
dote upon – *love a great deal (foolishly)*

betroth'd – *engaged*; ere – *before*
like a sickness – *as one does when one is sick*

Now I do wish it, love it, long for it,   175
And will for evermore be true to it.

THESEUS

Fair lovers, you are fortunately met;
Of this discourse we more will hear anon.
Egeus, I will overbear your will;
For in the temple, by and by, with us,   180
These couples shall eternally be knit.
And, for the morning now is something worn,
Our purpos'd hunting shall be set aside.
Away, with us, to Athens: three and three,
We'll hold a feast in great solemnity.   185
Come, Hippolyta.

Exeunt Theseus, Hippolyta, Egeus and train.

DEMETRIUS

These things seem small and undistinguishable,
Like far-off mountains turnèd into clouds.

HERMIA

Methinks I see these things with parted eye,
When everything seems double.

HELENA   So methinks;   190
And I have found Demetrius like a jewel,
Mine own, and not mine own.

DEMETRIUS   Are you sure
That we are awake? It seems to me
That yet we sleep, we dream. Do not you think
The Duke was here, and bid us follow him?   195

Q1 – I do Q2/F – do I

discourse – *subject*   Q1 – more will hear Q2 – will hear more F – shall hear more
overbear – *overrule*

knit – *joined together in marriage*
for – *since*; something – *somewhat*; worn – *spent*
purpos'd – *intended*
three and three – *three couples*
in – *with*; solemnity – *formal celebration*

Metre – line is short by 5 syl.

undinstinguishable – *difficult to make out*   **un**-dis-**ting**-guish-**able** (equiv. 5 syl.)

parted eye – *unfocused eyes*

Mine . . . own – *mine now but someone else's before (like in the saying 'finders keepers')*

Qq – Are . . . awake – not in F; Metre – this shared line is short by 1 syl.
Metre – line is headless (see 'A Note on Metre')
yet – *still*

HERMIA
Yea, and my father.

HELENA   And Hippolyta.

LYSANDER
And he did bid us follow to the temple.

DEMETRIUS
Why then, we are awake: let's follow him,
And by the way let us recount our dreams.   *Exeunt.*

BOTTOM
[*waking*] When my cue comes, call me and I will   200
answer. My next is 'Most fair Pyramus'. Heigh-ho!
Peter Quince? Flute, the bellows-mender? Snout,
the tinker? Starveling? God's my life! Stolen hence,
and left me asleep! I have had a most rare vision.
I have had a dream, past the wit of man to say what   205
dream it was. Man is but an ass if he go about to expound
this dream. Methought I was – there is no
man can tell what. Methought I was – and methought
I had – but man is but a patched fool if he
will offer to say what methought I had. The eye of   210
man hath not heard, the ear of man hath not seen,
man's hand is not able to taste, his tongue to conceive,
nor his heart to report, what my dream was. I
will get Peter Quince to write a ballad of this
dream: it shall be called 'Bottom's Dream', because   215
it hath no bottom; and I will sing it in the latter end
of a play, before the Duke. Peradventure, to make it
the more gracious, I shall sing it at her death.   *Exit.*

by – *on*

next – *next cue*; Heigh-ho! – *(a yawn)*

God's my life! – *Good lord!*; hence – *away from here*

Qq – have had F – had
wit of man – *power of the human mind*
go about – *try*; expound – *explain*
Methought – *I thought*

a ... fool – *a fool who traditionally wore a patched, mutli-coloured coat*
offer – *venture*; The ... report – (Bottom confuses the senses, misquoting the Bible
– 1 Corinthians 2.9–10)
conceive – *understand (with the heart)*

ballad – *a story set to a popular tune*

hath no bottom – *is unfathomable/ has no substance*; in ... end – *towards the end*
Peradventure – *Perhaps*
gracious – *appealing*; her – *Thisbe's*

ACT 4, SCENE 2

Enter QUINCE, FLUTE, SNOUT and STARVELING.

QUINCE

Have you sent to Bottom's house? Is he come
home yet?

STARVELING

He cannot be heard of. Out of doubt he is transported.

FLUTE

If he come not, then the play is marred: it goes not
forward, doth it?   5

QUINCE

It is not possible. You have not a man in all Athens able to
discharge Pyramus but he.

FLUTE

No, he hath simply the best wit of any handicraft
man in Athens.

QUINCE

Yea, and the best person too; and he is a very   10
paramour for a sweet voice.

FLUTE

You must say paragon. A paramour is, God bless
us, a thing of naught.

transported – *carried away/transformed*

marred – *ruined*
forward – *ahead*

discharge – *perform*

wit – *intellect*

person – *appearance*
paramour – *sexual partner (malapropism for paragon)*

paragon – *model*
thing of naught – *a shameful thing*

Enter SNUG *the joiner.*

SNUG

    Masters, the Duke is coming from the temple, and
    there is two or three lords and ladies more married.   15
    If our sport had gone forward, we had all been
    made men.

FLUTE

    O sweet bully Bottom! Thus hath he lost sixpence a
    day during his life; he could not have 'scaped sixpence
    a day. And the Duke had not given him sixpence   20
    a day for playing Pyramus, I'll be hanged.
    He would have deserved it: sixpence a day in Pyramus,
    or nothing.

Enter BOTTOM.

BOTTOM

    Where are these lads? Where are these hearts?

QUINCE

    Bottom! O most courageous day! O most happy   25
    hour!

BOTTOM

    Masters, I am to discourse wonders: but ask me not what;
    for if I tell you, I am not true Athenian. I will
    tell you everything, right as it fell out.

QUINCE

    Let us hear, sweet Bottom.   30

sport – *entertainment*
made men – *men with our fortunes made*

bully – *(term of endearment)*; sixpence . . . life – *(as a royal pension)*
'scaped – *escaped*
And – *If*

in – *for*

hearts – *mates*

courageous – *mistake for brave, meaning splendid*

right – *exactly*; fell out – *happened*

Qq – not F – no
Qq – right as F – as

BOTTOM

Not a word of me. All that I will tell you is, that the
Duke hath dined. Get your apparel together, good
strings to your beards, new ribbons to your pumps;
meet presently at the palace; every man look o'er
his part: for the short and the long is, our play is   35
preferred. In any case, let Thisbe have clean linen;
and let not him that plays the lion pare his nails, for
they shall hang out for the lion's claws. And most
dear actors, eat no onions nor garlic, for we are to
utter sweet breath; and I do not doubt but to hear   40
them say, it is a sweet comedy. No more words.
Away! Go, away!

Exeunt.

ACT 5, SCENE 1

Enter THESEUS, HIPPOLYTA; *lords and attendants, among them*
PHILOSTRATE.

HIPPOLYTA

'Tis strange, my Theseus, that these lovers speak of.

THESEUS

More strange than true. I never may believe
These antique fables, nor these fairy toys.
Lovers and madmen have such seething brains,
Such shaping fantasies, that apprehend   5
More than cool reason ever comprehends.
The lunatic, the lover, and the poet
Are of imagination all compact:
One sees more devils than vast hell can hold;
That is the madman: the lover, all as frantic,   10

of – *out of*
apparel – *clothing/costumes*
strings – *(to tie false beards on)*; pumps – *light shoes*
presently – *shortly*; o'er – *over*

preferred – *recommended*
pare – *cut*

F has Egeus enter instead of Philostrate and speak his lines in this scene,
but this makes little sense (see Introduction).

that – *that which*

antique – *old/strange*; toys – *trifles*   Q1 – antique Q2/F – anticke
seething – *boiling*
fantasies – *imaginations*; apprehend – *grasp*

all compact – *entirely made up*

all – *just*   man: the **lov**- (anapest – see 'A Note on Metre')

Sees Helen's beauty in a brow of Egypt:
The poet's eye, in a fine frenzy rolling,
Doth glance from heaven to earth, from earth to heaven;
And as imagination bodies forth
The forms of things unknown, the poet's pen   15
Turns them to shapes, and gives to airy nothing
A local habitation and a name.
Such tricks hath strong imagination,
That if it would but apprehend some joy,
It comprehends some bringer of that joy: 20
Or, in the night, imagining some fear,
How easy is a bush suppos'd a bear!

HIPPOLYTA

But all the story of the night told over,
And all their minds transfigur'd so together,
More witnesseth than fancy's images,   25
And grows to something of great constancy;
But howsoever, strange and admirable.

Enter the lovers: LYSANDER, DEMETRIUS, HERMIA *and* HELENA.

THESEUS

Here come the lovers, full of joy and mirth.
Joy, gentle friends, joy and fresh days of love
Accompany your hearts!

LYSANDER   More than to us   30
Wait in your royal walks, your board, your bed!

THESEUS

Come now; what masques, what dances shall we have,
To wear away this long age of three hours
Between our after-supper and bed-time?

Helen's . . . Egypt – *the beauty of Helen of Troy in the face of a gypsy* (see Myth)

heaven (equiv. 1 syl.)

bodies forth – *gives shape to*

local habitation – *location*

Metre suggests i-**mag**-i-**nat**-i-**on** (equiv. 6 syl.)

apprehend – *perceive*
bringer – *source*
fear – *fearful object*
easy – *easily*

told over – *recited*   over (equiv. 1 syl.)
transfigur'd so together – *changed in the same way*
More . . . images – *suggests something more than mere imagination*
constancy – *consistency*
howsoever – *in any case*; admirable – *wondrous*   **ad**-mira-**ble** (equiv. 3 syl.)

mirth – *happiness*

More than – *more joy than you wish*
Wait – *Attend you*; board – *table*

masques – *courtly entertainments*

after-supper – *dessert*

Where is our usual manager of mirth?   35
What revels are in hand? Is there no play
To ease the anguish of a torturing hour?
Call Philostrate.

PHILOSTRATE
  [*advancing*]   Here, mighty Theseus.

THESEUS
  Say, what abridgement have you for this evening,
  What masque, what music? How shall we beguile   40
  The lazy time, if not with some delight?

PHILOSTRATE
  There is a brief how many sports are ripe:
  Make choice of which your Highness will see first.
  [*giving a paper*]

THESEUS
  [*Reads.*] *The battle with the Centaurs, to be sung*
  By an Athenian eunuch to the harp?   45
  We'll none of that; that have I told my love
  In glory of my kinsman Hercules.
  [*Reads.*] *The riot of the tipsy Bacchanals,*
  Tearing the Thracian singer in their rage?
  That is an old device, and it was play'd   50
  When I from Thebes came last a conqueror.
  [*Reads.*] *The thrice three Muses mourning for the death*
  Of learning, late deceas'd in beggary?
  That is some satire, keen and critical,
  Not sorting with a nuptial ceremony.   55
  [*Reads.*] *A tedious brief scene of young Pyramus*
  And his love Thisbe, very tragical mirth?
  Merry and tragical? Tedious and brief?

manager of mirth – *Master of Revels*

tor-turing (equiv. 2 syl.)

abridgement – *pastime;* beguile – *cheat*

brief – *short list;* ripe – *ready*   In F the paper is given to Lysander to read.

F – 'The … harp' – spoken by Lysander
Centaurs (see Myth)   Source: Ovid, *Metamorphosis,* Book XII
eunuch – *castrated male*   Q1 question marks suggest – 'what about this?'

Theseus and Hercules were cousins. Source: Plutarch
tipsy – *drunken;* Bacchanals – *female followers of the God Dionysus* (see Myth)
Thracian singer – *Orpheus* (see Myth)   F – 'The … rage' – spoken by Lysander
device – *drama*

thrice three – *nine*   F – 'The … beggary' – spoken by Lysander
late – *recently*
keen – *sharp*
sorting with – *befitting*   **cere**-mon-y (equiv. 3 syl.)
    F – 'A tedious … mirth' – spoken by Lysander; **te**-dious (equiv. 2 syl.)

Te-dious (equiv. 2 syl.)

That is hot ice, and wondrous strange snow!
How shall we find the concord of this discord?   60

PHILOSTRATE
A play there is, my lord, some ten words long,
Which is as brief as I have known a play;
But by ten words, my lord, it is too long,
Which makes it tedious; for in all the play
There is not one word apt, one player fitted.   65
And tragical, my noble lord, it is,
For Pyramus therein doth kill himself;
Which, when I saw rehears'd, I must confess
Made mine eyes water; but more merry tears
The passion of loud laughter never shed.   70

THESEUS
What are they that do play it?

PHILOSTRATE
Hard-handed men that work in Athens here,
Which never labour'd in their minds till now;
And now have toil'd their unbreath'd memories
With this same play, against your nuptial.   75

THESEUS
And we will hear it.

PHILOSTRATE   No, my noble lord,
It is not for you: I have heard it over,
And it is nothing, nothing in the world;
Unless you can find sport in their intents,
Extremely stretch'd and conn'd with cruel pain   80
To do you service.

strange – *unnatural*   **won**-d-**rous** (equiv. 3 syl.); editors expecting an oxymoron
concord – *agreement*   emend to 'black snow'

                                                    te-dious (equiv. 2 syl.)
fitted – *appropriately cast*

                                        Metre – this line is short by 3 syl.

toil'd – *taxed*; unbreath'd – *unexercised*
against – *in preparation for*   **nup**-ti-**al** (equiv. 3 syl.)

sport – *entertainment*
stretch'd – *strained*; conn'd – *memorized*

THESEUS   I will hear that play;
　　For never anything can be amiss
　　When simpleness and duty tender it.
　　Go bring them in; and take your places, ladies.

[Exit Philostrate.]

HIPPOLYTA
　　I love not to see wretchedness o'er-charg'd,   85
　　And duty in his service perishing.

THESEUS
　　Why, gentle sweet, you shall see no such thing.

HIPPOLYTA
　　He says they can do nothing in this kind.

THESEUS
　　The kinder we, to give them thanks for nothing.
　　Our sport shall be to take what they mistake: 90
　　And what poor duty cannot do, noble respect
　　Takes it in might, not merit.
　　Where I have come, great clerks have purposed
　　To greet me with premeditated welcomes;
　　Where I have seen them shiver and look pale,   95
　　Make periods in the midst of sentences,
　　Throttle their practis'd accent in their fears,
　　And, in conclusion, dumbly have broke off,
　　Not paying me a welcome. Trust me, sweet,
　　Out of this silence yet I pick'd a welcome,   100
　　And in the modesty of fearful duty
　　I read as much as from the rattling tongue
　　Of saucy and audacious eloquence.

amiss – *wrong*
tender – *offer*

o'er-charg'd – *overstretched*
in his service – *in its attempts to serve*

in this kind – *of this sort*

sport – *entertainment*; take – *accept*
respect – *consideration*   Metre – irregular lines. Line 91 is 12 syls and
in . . . merit – *according to effort not results*   line 92 is 7 syls (see Intro.)
clerks – *scholars*
premeditated – *carefully thought out*

periods – *full stops*   **pe**-riods (equiv. 2 syl.)
practis'd accents – *elocutionary technique*; in – *as a result of*
dumbly – *without words*

pick'd – *discerned*
modesty – *deference*; fearful – *frightened*

                    ratt-ling (equiv. 2 syl.)

saucy – *presumptious*; audacious – *bold*

Love, therefore, and tongue-tied simplicity
In least speak most, to my capacity.   105

[Enter PHILOSTRATE.*]*

PHILOSTRATE
So please your grace, the Prologue is address'd.

THESEUS
Let him approach.

[Flourish of trumpets.] Enter QUINCE *for the* PROLOGUE.

PROLOGUE
If we offend, it is with our good will.
That you should think, we come not to offend,
But with good will. To show our simple skill,   110
That is the true beginning of our end.
Consider then, we come but in despite.
We do not come, as minding to content you,
Our true intent is. All for your delight,
We are not here. That you should here repent you,   115
The actors are at hand; and by their show,
You shall know all, that you are like to know.

THESEUS
This fellow doth not stand upon points.

LYSANDER
He hath rid his prologue like a rough colt; he knows not
the stop. A good moral, my lord: it is not enough   120
to speak, but to speak true.

to my capacity – *in my judgement*

address'd – *ready to begin*

Metre – this line is short by 6 syl.

The punctuation of this speech indicates Quince's mispunctuation in his delivery.

end – *aim*
despite – *scorn*
minding – *intending*
All – *Exclusively*

like – *likely*

stand upon points – *take notice of the punctuation*   Theseus, Hippolyta and
the lovers speak in prose during the Mechanicals' play

rough – *unbroken*; colt – *young wild horse*
the stop – *the punctuation/how to stop the horse*

HIPPOLYTA

Indeed he hath played on this prologue like a child on a
recorder; a sound, but not in government.

THESEUS

His speech was like a tangled chain; nothing impaired,
but all disordered. Who is next?   125

Enter, with a trumpeter before them, [BOTTOM as]
PYRAMUS, [FLUTE as] THISBE, [SNOUT as] WALL,
[STARVELING as] MOONSHINE and [SNUG as] LION.

PROLOGUE

Gentles, perchance you wonder at this show;
But wonder on, till truth make all things plain.
This man is Pyramus, if you would know;
This beauteous lady Thisbe is certain.
This man, with lime and rough-cast, doth present   130
Wall, that vile wall which did these lovers sunder;
And through Wall's chink, poor souls, they are content
To whisper. At the which let no man wonder.
This man, with lantern, dog, and bush of thorn,
Presenteth Moonshine; for, if you will know,   135
By moonshine did these lovers think no scorn
To meet at Ninus' tomb, there, there to woo.
This grisly beast, which Lion hight by name,
The trusty Thisbe, coming first by night,
Did scare away, or rather did affright;   140
And as she fled, her mantle she did fall,
Which Lion vile with bloody mouth did stain.
Anon comes Pyramus, sweet youth and tall,
And finds his trusty Thisbe's mantle slain;
Whereat with blade, with bloody blameful blade,   145

Qq – this F – his

recorder – *musical pipe instrument*; government – *control*

nothing – *not at all*

SD – the actors enter for a dumb show (silent mime of the action), performed during the Prologue

perchance – *perhaps*   The Prologue is spoken by Quince.
make – *makes*

certain – Pron. – metre and rhyme suggest this should be pronounced cer-**tain**
rough-cast – *coarse plaster surface*   (to rhyme with plain)
sunder – *separate*

no scorn – *it no disgrace*
Ninus – (see Myth)   Ninus – Pron. – **Nine**-us
hight – *is called*

mantle – *loose sleeveless cloak*; fall – *let drop*

tall – *fine/ brave*

He bravely broach'd his boiling bloody breast;
And Thisbe, tarrying in mulberry shade,
His dagger drew, and died. For all the rest.
Let Lion, Moonshine, Wall, and lovers twain
At large discourse, while here they do remain.   150

Exeunt Prologue, Pyramus, Thisbe, Lion and Moonshine.

THESEUS
I wonder if the lion be to speak?

DEMETRIUS
No wonder, my lord; one lion may when many asses do.

WALL
In this same interlude it doth befall
That I, one Snout by name, present a wall;
And such a wall as I would have you think   155
That had in it a crannied hole, or chink,
Through which the lovers, Pyramus and Thisbe,
Did whisper often, very secretly.
This loam, this rough-cast, and this stone doth show
That I am that same wall; the truth is so: 160
And this the cranny is, right and sinister,
Through which the fearful lovers are to whisper.

THESEUS
Would you desire lime and hair to speak better?

DEMETRIUS
It is the wittiest partition that ever I heard
discourse, my lord.   165

broach'd – *stabbed*

tarrying – *waiting*; in mulberry shade – *in the shade of a mulberry*   **tarry**-ing
(equiv. 2 syl.)

twain – *two/ separated*

large – *length*

be – *is going*

interlude – *play*

loam – *clay*; rough-cast – *rough plaster*

sinister – *left*

      Snout might make some effort to make sinister and whisper near rhymes.

hair – *animal hair (added to lime plaster for strength)*

wittiest – *most intelligent*; partition – *wall/part of an oration*

discourse – *speak*

Enter PYRAMUS.

THESEUS

    Pyramus draws near the wall; silence!

PYRAMUS

    O grim-look'd night! O night with hue so black!
    O night, which ever art when day is not!
    O night, O night, alack, alack, alack,
    I fear my Thisbe's promise is forgot!   170
    And thou, O wall, O sweet, O lovely wall,
    That stand'st between her father's ground and mine;
    Thou wall, O wall, O sweet and lovely wall,
    Show me thy chink, to blink through with mine eyne.

        [Wall stretches out his fingers.]

    Thanks, courteous wall: Jove shield thee well for this!   175
    But what see I? No Thisbe do I see.
    O wicked wall, through whom I see no bliss,
    Curs'd thy stones for thus deceiving me!

THESEUS

    The wall, methinks, being sensible, should curse
    again.   180

PYRAMUS

    No, in truth sir, he should not. 'Deceiving me' is
    Thisbe's cue: she is to enter now, and I am to spy
    her through the wall. You shall see it will fall pat as
    I told you: yonder she comes.

grim-look'd – *grim-looking*; hue – *colour*

Q1 – stand'st Q2/F – stands

eyne – *eye*

Jove – (see Myth)   **cour**-teous (equiv. 2 syl.)

stones – *(pun on testicles)*

sensible – *capable of feeling*
again – *back*

pat – *precisely*

Enter THISBE.

THISBE
> O wall, full often hast thou heard my moans,   185
> For parting my fair Pyramus and me!
> My cherry lips have often kiss'd thy stones,
> Thy stones with lime and hair knit up in thee.

PYRAMUS
> I see a voice; now will I to the chink,
> To spy and I can hear my Thisbe's face.   190
> Thisbe?

THISBE   *My love thou art, my love I think!*

PYRAMUS
> Think what thou wilt, I am thy lover's grace;
> And like Limander am I trusty still.

THISBE
> And I like Helen, till the Fates me kill.

PYRAMUS
> Not Shafalus to Procrus was so true.   195

THISBE
> As Shafalus to Procrus, I to you.

PYRAMUS
> O kiss me through the hole of this vile wall.

THISBE
> I kiss the wall's hole, not your lips at all.

stones – *(again a pun on testicles)*
knit ... thee – *bound together*

and – *if*

Thisbe mispunctuates the line.

lover's grace – *gracious lover*
Limander (Li-**man**-der)– *(error for Leander)* (see Myth)

Helen – *(error for Hero)* (see Myth); Fates – (see Myth)

Shafalus (**Shaff**-a-**lus**) – *(error for Cephalus)*; Procrus (**Prok**-rus) – *(error for Procris)* (see Myth)

hole – *(play on anus)*

PYRAMUS
　　Wilt thou at Ninny's tomb meet me straightway?

THISBE
　　'Tide life, 'tide death, I come without delay.　　　　　200

　　　　　Exeunt Pyramus and Thisbe, [severally.]

WALL
　　Thus have I, Wall, my part dischargèd so;
　　And, being done, thus Wall away doth go.

　　　　　Exit.

THESEUS
　　Now is the mure rased between the two neighbours.

DEMETRIUS
　　No remedy my lord, when walls are so wilful
　　to hear without warning.　　　　　205

HIPPOLYTA
　　This is the silliest stuff that ever I heard.

THESEUS
　　The best in this kind are but shadows; and the
　　worst are no worse, if imagination amend them.

HIPPOLYTA
　　It must be your imagination then, and not theirs.

THESEUS
　　If we imagine no worse of them than they of　　　　　210
　　themselves, they may pass for excellent men. Here come
　　two noble beasts in, a man and a lion.

'Tide – *Betide/Come*

mure – *wall*; rased – *down*   Brooks – mure rased F – morall downe Pope – wall down

wilful – *forward*; when . . . warning – Prov. – *walls have ears*
to – *as to*

Q1 – ever Q2/F – ere

kind – *profession*; shadows – *images/actors*
amend – *correct*

Enter LION *and* MOONSHINE.

LION

You ladies, you whose gentle hearts do fear
The smallest monstrous mouse that creeps on floor,
May now, perchance, both quake and tremble here,   215
When lion rough in wildest rage doth roar.
Then know that I as Snug the joiner am
A lion fell, nor else no lion's dam;
For if I should as lion come in strife
Into this place, 'twere pity on my life.   220

THESEUS

A very gentle beast, and of a good conscience.

DEMETRIUS

The very best at a beast, my lord, that e'er I saw.

LYSANDER

This lion is a very fox for his valour.

THESEUS

True; and a goose for his discretion.

DEMETRIUS

Not so, my lord, for his valour cannot carry his   225
discretion; and the fox carries the goose.

THESEUS

His discretion, I am sure, cannot carry his valour;
for the goose carries not the fox. It is well: leave it to
his discretion, and let us listen to the moon.

mon-strous (equiv. 2 syl.)

perchance – *perhaps*

Qq – as F – one

fell – *fierce*; dam – *mother*

Qq – on F – of

at – *at playing*

fox – *(symbol of low cunning rather than courage)*

goose – *(symbol of foolishness)*; discretion – *judgement*

his valour ... discretion – *he is not brave enough to be wise*

his discretion ... valour – *he is not wise enough to be brave*

Q1 – listen Q2/F – hearken

MOONSHINE
This lantern doth the hornèd moon present –   230

DEMETRIUS
He should have worn the horns on his head.

THESEUS
He is no crescent, and his horns are invisible within
the circumference.

MOONSHINE
This lantern doth the hornèd moon present;
Myself the Man i'th' Moon do seem to be.   235

THESEUS
This is the greatest error of all the rest; the man
should be put into the lantern. How is it else the Man
i'the Moon?

DEMETRIUS
He dares not come there for the candle; for you see
it is already in snuff.   240

HIPPOLYTA
I am aweary of this moon. Would he would change!

THESEUS
It appears by his small light of discretion that he is
in the wane; but yet in courtesy, in all reason, we
must stay the time.

LYSANDER
Proceed, Moon.   245

hornèd – *crescent*

horns ... head – *(the symbol of a cuckold)*

no crescent – *no growing moon (possibly a reference to Starveling's thinness)*
circumference – *circle of the moon*

Qq – do F – doth

in snuff – *in need of being extinguished/ angry*

Q1 – aweary Q2/F – weary

in the wane – *decreasing*; in all reason – *it is only reasonable*
stay the time – *sit it out*

MOONSHINE
> All that I have to say is, to tell you that the lantern
> is the moon; I the Man i'th' Moon; this thorn-bush
> my thorn-bush; and this dog my dog.

DEMETRIUS
> Why, all these should be in the lantern, for all
> these are in the moon. But silence: here comes Thisbe. 250

Enter THISBE.

THISBE
> *This is old Ninny's tomb. Where is my love?*

LION
> *O – !*

The Lion roars. Thisbe, [dropping her mantle], runs off.

DEMETRIUS
> Well roared, Lion!

THESEUS
> Well run, Thisbe!

HIPPOLYTA
> Well shone, Moon! Truly, the moon shines with a 255
> good grace.

[The Lion worries the mantle, and exit.]

THESEUS
> Well moused, Lion!

Qq – i'th' F – in the

Q1 – for all these Q2/F – for they

moused – *(in treating the mantle like a cat treats a mouse)*

DEMETRIUS
    And then came Pyramus –

LYSANDER
    And so the lion vanished.

            Enter PYRAMUS.

PYRAMUS
    Sweet Moon, I thank thee for thy sunny beams;   260
    I thank thee, Moon, for shining now so bright;
    For by thy gracious, golden, glittering gleams,
    I trust to take of truest Thisbe sight.
    But stay! O spite!
    But mark, poor knight,   265
    What dreadful dole is here?
    Eyes, do you see?
    How can it be?
    O dainty duck! O dear!
    Thy mantle good,   270
    What! Stain'd with blood?
    Approach, ye Furies fell!
    O Fates, come, come!
    Cut thread and thrum:
    Quail, crush, conclude, and quell.   275

THESEUS
    This passion, and the death of a dear friend, would
    go near to make a man look sad.

HIPPOLYTA
    Beshrew my heart, but I pity the man.

glitt-ering (equiv. 2 syl.); Staunton – gleams Qq/F – beams
Qq – take F – taste; Qq – Thisbe F – Thisbies
Metre – the end of the speech is in ballad metre – see Intro. –
The Metre of Pyramus and Thisbe

dole – *sorrow*

Furies – *classical goddesses of vengeance* (see Myth); fell – *fierce*   Qq – ye F – you
Fates – *the three classical goddesses of destiny* (see Myth)
thrum – *tufted end on a weaver's loom*
Quail – *overpower;* quell – *slay*

go near to – *almost*

Beshrew – *Curse*

PYRAMUS

> *O wherefore, Nature, didst thou lions frame,*
> *Since lion vile hath here deflower'd my dear?*   280
> *Which is – no, no – which was the fairest dame*
> *That liv'd, that lov'd, that lik'd, that look'd with cheer.*
> *Come tears, confound!*
> *Out sword, and wound*
> *The pap of Pyramus;*   285
> *Ay, that left pap,*
> *Where heart doth hop:* [*Stabs himself.*]
> *Thus die I, thus, thus, thus!*
> *Now am I dead,*
> *Now am I fled;*   290
> *My soul is in the sky.*
> *Tongue, lose thy light;*
> *Moon, take thy flight!* [*Exit Moonshine.*]
> *Now die, die, die, die, die.* [*Dies.*]

DEMETRIUS

> No die, but an ace for him; for he is but one.   295

LYSANDER

> Less than an ace, man; for he is dead, he is nothing.

THESEUS

> With the help of a surgeon he might yet recover,
> and prove an ass.

HIPPOLYTA

> How chance Moonshine is gone, before Thisbe
> comes back and finds her lover?   300

frame – *create*
deflower'd – *(malapropism for devoured)*

cheer – *face/joy*

Metre – the rest of the speech is in ballad metre – see Intro. –
The Metre of Pyramus and Thisbe

pap – *breast*

Tongue – *(error for eye)*

die – *pair of dice*; ace – *one spot on a dice*

Q2/F – prove Q1 – yet prove

chance – *come*

THESEUS
    She will find him by starlight.

Enter THISBE.

    Here she comes, and her passion ends the play.

HIPPOLYTA
    Methinks she should not use a long one for such a
    Pyramus; I hope she will be brief.

DEMETRIUS
    A mote will turn the balance, which Pyramus,   305
    which Thisbe, is the better: he for a man, God warrant
    us; she for a woman, God bless us!

LYSANDER
    She hath spied him already with those sweet eyes.

DEMETRIUS
    And thus she means, videlicet –

THISBE
    Asleep, my love?   310
    What, dead, my dove?
    O Pyramus, arise!
    Speak, speak! Quite dumb?
    Dead, dead? A tomb
    Must cover thy sweet eyes.   315
    These lily lips,
    This cherry nose,
    These yellow cowslip cheeks,
    Are gone, are gone!

passion – *suffereing/passionate speech*

long one – *long fit of grief*

mote – *tiny particle*
warrant – *preserve*   Qq – he . . . us! – Not in F

means – *moans/laments*; videlicit – *that is to say (Latin)*

Metre – these lines are in ballad metre – see Introduction – The Metre of
Pyramus and Thisbe

Lovers, make moan; 320
His eyes were green as leeks.
O Sisters Three,
Come, come to me,
With hands as pale as milk;
Lay them in gore, 325
Since you have shore
With shears his thread of silk.
Tongue, not a word:
Come, trusty sword,
Come, blade, my breast imbrue! [*Stabs herself.*] 330
And farewell, friends;
Thus Thisbe ends:
Adieu, adieu, adieu! [*Dies.*]

THESEUS
Moonshine and Lion are left to bury the dead.

DEMETRIUS
Ay, and Wall too. 335

BOTTOM
[*starting up*] No, I assure you; the wall is down that
parted their fathers. [*Flute rises.*] Will it please you to
see the epilogue, or to hear a Bergomask dance
between two of our company?

THESEUS
No epilogue, I pray you; for your play needs no 340
excuse. Never excuse; for when the players are all
dead, there need none to be blamed. Marry, if he
that writ it had played Pyramus, and hanged himself
in Thisbe's garter, it would have been a fine

Sisters Three – *the Fates* (see Myth)

thread of silk – *life*

imbrue – *pierce*

left – *left alive*

Bergomask dance – *rustic dance (in manner of the people of Bergamo)*
between – *performed by*

Qq – hanged F – hung; hanged ... garter – Prov.

tragedy – and so it is, truly, and very notably discharged. 345
But come, your Bergomask; let your
epilogue alone.

[Enter QUINCE, SNUG, SNOUT *and* STARVELING *two of
whom dance a bergamask. Then exeunt handicraftsmen,
including Flute and Bottom.]*

The iron tongue of midnight hath told twelve.
Lovers, to bed; 'tis almost fairy time.
I fear we shall outsleep the coming morn   350
As much as we this night have overwatch'd.
This palpable-gross play hath well beguil'd
The heavy gait of night. Sweet friends, to bed.
A fortnight hold we this solemnity
In nightly revels and new jollity.   355

Exeunt

Enter PUCK.

PUCK
Now the hungry lion roars,
And the wolf behowls the moon;
Whilst the heavy ploughman snores,
All with weary task fordone.
Now the wasted brands do glow,   360
Whilst the screech-owl, screeching loud,
Puts the wretch that lies in woe
In remembrance of a shroud.
Now it is the time of night
That the graves, all gaping wide,   365
Every one lets forth his sprite

iron tongue – *clapper of a bell*; told – *counted*   Theseus speaks in VERSE again

overwatch'd – *stayed up late*
palpable-gross – *obviously uncouth*; beguil'd – *whiled away*
heavy gait – *slow walk*
solemnity – *celebration*

Metre – final speeches are in catalectic trochaic tetrameter – see Intro. – Magic Metre
Theobald – behowls Qq/F – beholds
heavy – *tired*
fordone – *tired*
wasted brands – *logs, almost burnt-out*
screech-owl – *barn owl (whose screech was thought to be a bad omen)*

sprite – *spirit*

In the church-way paths to glide.
And we fairies, that do run
By the triple Hecate's team
From the presence of the sun,   370
Following darkness like a dream,
Now are frolic; not a mouse
Shall disturb this hallow'd house.
I am sent with broom before
To sweep the dust behind the door.   375

Enter OBERON *and* TITANIA, *the King and Queen of*
Fairies, with all their train.

OBERON

Through the house give glimmering light
By the dead and drowsy fire;
Every elf and fairy sprite
Hop as light as bird from briar;
And this ditty after me   380
Sing, and dance it trippingly.

TITANIA

First rehearse your song by rote,
To each word a warbling note;
Hand in hand, with fairy grace,
Will we sing, and bless this place.   385

[Oberon leading, the Fairies sing and dance.]

OBERON

Now, until the break of day,
Through this house each fairy stray.
To the best bride-bed will we,

Hecate (**He**-cate (2 syl.) – (see Myth)

Foll-owing (equiv. 2 syl.)

frolic – *frolicsome*
hallow'd – *blessed*
broom – *(attribute of Robin Goodfellow)*
behind – *from behind*

glimm-ering (equiv. 2 syl.)

trippingly – *skilfully/lightly*

rehearse – *recite*; by rote – *by memory*   Q1 – your Q2/F – this
warbling – *quavering/tuneful*

Titania sings the remainder of the speech in F.

best bride-bed – *(that of Theseus and Hippolyta)*

Which by us shall blessèd be;
And the issue there create   390
Ever shall be fortunate.
So shall all the couples three
Ever true in loving be;
And the blots of Nature's hand
Shall not in their issue stand: 395
Never mole, hare-lip, nor scar,
Nor mark prodigious, such as are
Despisèd in nativity,
Shall upon their children be.
With this field-dew consecrate,   400
Every fairy take his gait,
And each several chamber bless
Through this palace with sweet peace;
And the owner of it blest,
Ever shall in safety rest.   405
Trip away; make no stay;
Meet me all by break of day.

Exeunt [all but Puck.]

PUCK
[*to the audience*] If we shadows have offended,
Think but this, and all is mended,
That you have but slumber'd here   410
While these visions did appear.
And this weak and idle theme,
No more yielding but a dream,
Gentles, do not reprehend:
If you pardon, we will mend.   415
And, as I am an honest Puck,
If we have unearnèd luck

issue – *children*; create – *created*

mark prodigious – *portentous birth mark*

consecrate – *blessed*
take his gait – *go on his way*
several – *individual*

stay – *delay*   Metre – This line is missing one beat at the caesura.

shadows – *fairies/ actors*

slumber'd – *slept*

weak – *deficient*; idle – *foolish*
yielding but – *meaningful than*
Gentles – *ladies and gentlemen*; reprehend – *reprove*
mend – *do better in future*

unearnèd – *undeserved*

Now to 'scape the serpent's tongue,
We will make amends ere long;
Else the Puck a liar call.   420
So, goodnight unto you all.
Give me your hands, if we be friends,
And Robin shall restore amends.   [*Exit.*]

'scape – *escape*; serpent's tongue – *hissing (from the audience)*
ere – *before*

Give me your hands – *applaud*
restore amends – *make amends in return*